# No Other Gods

# NO OTHER GODS

*The Modern Struggle
Against Idolatry*

**Kenneth Seeskin**

**BEHRMAN HOUSE, INC.**

Copyright © 1995 Kenneth Seeskin


Published by Behrman House, Inc.
235 Watchung Ave.
West Orange, NJ 07052


Book design by Richard Stalzer Associates, Ltd.

---

Library of Congress Cataloging-in-Publication Data

Seeskin, Kenneth, 1947–
     No other gods : the continuing struggle against idolatry / by
    Kenneth Seeskin.
           p.   cm.
    Includes bibliographical references.
    ISBN 0-87441-583-7
    1. Idolatry.  2. Idols and images—Worship.  3. Ten
    commandments—Other gods.  4. God (Judaism)   I. Title.
    BL485.S47    1995
    296.3´1—dc20                  95-10661
                                        CIP

---

Manufactured in the United States of America

6  5  4  3  2  1
98  97  96  95

To Elizabeth

*Philosopher from the day she was born*

# Contents

# Preface

The idea for this book came to me several years ago when I was teaching a confirmation class at a synagogue in Chicago. On the first day of class, I asked the students to write their own ten commandments. The instructions were simple: "Don't worry about Moses' ten commandments; I want to know what *you* regard as the most basic principles for how to live." Given the age of the students, it is understandable that no one came up with a commandment that read: "Honor thy father and mother." And it is understandable why there were commandments dealing with homework, use of the family car, and weekly allowances. But to my great surprise, no one had a commandment prohibiting idol worship. When I asked if the problem was that no one believed in God, I was told that belief in God has nothing to do with it: the students believed in God; they simply saw no reason why bowing to images of God is objectionable.

I remember thinking that if this response is typical of post–Bar and Bat Mitzvah students, something is terribly wrong. Have they spent so much time singing, dancing, walking for Israel, looking at Holocaust films, and speed-reading Torah portions that they have neglected the single most important feature of the religion? Can they understand why countless martyrs went to their death rather than kneel to a piece of clay? Sadly, I came to see that the answer to the first question is yes, and the second one no. And even more sadly, I came to see that what was true of the students was also true of their parents. This book represents my attempt to focus attention on Judaism's main contribution to world culture: the first and second commandments.

As usual, I wish to thank the people who read drafts, provoked discussion, pointed out mistakes, listened to problems, and offered moral support. They are Joseph Edelheit, David Novak, Menachem Kellner, and Julie P. Gordon. With a backup system like this, I am among the most fortunate of authors.

With certain modifications, all biblical citations are taken from the Jewish Publication Society edition of the Holy Scriptures. Citations from Maimonides' *Guide of the Perplexed* are taken from the Pines translation published by the University of Chicago Press.

# NO OTHER GODS

# CHAPTER ONE

# Why Idolatry Is Alive and Well

Whoever acknowledges idolatry disavows the whole Torah, and whoever disavows idolatry acknowledges the whole Torah.

Sifre Deuteronomy 28

# ▣ The Litmus Test of Judaism

To many outsiders, and to some insiders as well, Judaism seems like an endlessly complicated religion. There are 613 commandments in the Torah governing everything from morality to social relations, from work to rest, from the food people put in their mouths to the clothes they put on their bodies. Centuries of interpretation and exposition have produced additional rules dealing with prayer, birth and death, marriage and divorce, charity, study, healing, in short, almost every aspect of human life. So it is hardly surprising if a person looks at the religion and asks a simple question: What are all of these rules for? Why does it matter if a person prays, fasts, rests on Shabbat, and eats kosher food?

The usual answer is that reduced to barest essentials, Judaism is a way of life summed up by the first two commandments: acceptance of God and rejection of idolatry. According to the quotation at the beginning of this chapter, the prohibition against idolatry is so important that it is equal in weight to the entire Torah. A well-known tradition expands on this insight by claiming that all the other commandments were given to Moses and passed on to the rest of the people but that when God issued the first two commandments, everyone at Sinai became a prophet and heard the voice directly.[1] There is even a tradition that holds that anyone who rejects idolatry is considered a Jew.[2]

Clearly the first two commandments are related: to accept God is to reject all competitors. It could be said, therefore, that idolatry is the litmus test for being a Jew: renounce it and you are part of the faith community that descends from Abraham; accept it and you are not. So to understand Judaism we must ask what idolatry is and why it is worth embarking on a way of life designed to avoid it. In simple terms, we have to ask what is behind the prayer that Jews say every day of their life and that countless martyrs have said before their death: "Hear, O Israel, the Lord our God, the Lord is one."

There is no better place to begin than with the words that all Israel heard at the foot of Mount Sinai:

> *I am the Lord thy God, who brought thee out of the land of Egypt, out of the house of bondage.*
> *Thou shalt have no other gods before Me. Thou shalt not make unto thee a graven image, nor any manner of likeness, of any thing that is in heaven above, or that is in the earth beneath, or that is in the water under the earth; thou shalt not bow down to them or serve them; for I the Lord thy God am a jealous God . . . .*

The meaning seems clear. If there is only one God, there is only one thing in the universe worthy of worship and adoration; everything else is part of the created order and subject to the will of God. In fact, the division between God and creation is so decisive that not only are heavenly bodies, mortal creatures, and sea monsters not divine, they cannot even serve as images of the divine. Note, for example, that the English word *idol* is derived from the Greek word *eidolon,* which means image or likeness.

If Judaism speaks with a single voice on the evils of idolatry, it does not speak with a single voice on what idolatry is. In fact, its understanding of idolatry has changed considerably as social conditions and intellectual currents have changed. The second commandment was written at a time when people believed in the power of graven images and treated them with respect. The fact that the prophets rail against idols on page after page shows how strong the attraction of these idols must have been. But eventually graven images began to lose their appeal. By the rabbinic period, the prevailing opinion was that the lure of idolatry had been uprooted from Israel during the time of the Second Temple.[3] Since Judaism is committed to the rejection of idolatry, its understanding of the problem had to change.[4] Instead of bowing to graven images, idolatry came to mean drunkenness, sexual license, or other immoral practices associated with the Greco-Roman world. The difference in meaning is significant, because in the biblical period idolatry was interpreted as a sign of Israel's unfaithfulness, and thus the prophets often compared it to prostitution or marital infidelity.[5] In the rabbinic period, however, it became a sign of the ignorance and brutish nature of other peoples. The solution was to avoid eating other peoples' foods, drinking their wines, and associating with them more than necessary.

For Maimonides and the medieval philosophers, the problem is not bowing to a graven image that you have made with your hands but rather believing in an image of God that you have concocted in your mind. Thus a person who walks into a synagogue and prays to the image of a man on a throne is no better than the people who walked into pagan temples and prayed to statues of Zeus.[6] Maimonides admits that the Bible often describes God in human terms. We are told, for example, that Noah walked with God (Genesis 6:9) and that Moses spoke with God face to face (Exodus 33:11). He insists, however, that these and similar passages are parables or metaphors that cannot be taken literally. In a word, literal interpretation is tantamount to sin. The fault has nothing to do with being Jewish or gentile: it is part of the normal human tendency to regard spatial/temporal objects as the only reality. In Maimonides' opinion, every ritual, holiday, dietary law, and precept is designed to fight this tendency.

Although many people still think of God as a man on a throne, idolatry in the modern age is generally considered a moral error rather than an intellectual one. If God is the only thing in the universe worthy of worship or adoration, then anyone who becomes obsessed with the desire for wealth, beauty, fame, or power is said to *idolize* them. From a modern perspective then, idolatry is a universal phenomenon. Almost every country in the world has military parades that glorify power, advertisements that glorify beauty or sexual fulfillment, books that extol wealth or influence, and cults that deify movie stars and sports figures. Thus a person who devotes several hours a day to grooming, dressing, or body-building is said to "bow" to the god of fame or beauty even though he or she may live in a secular culture.

Even if we move from a secular context to a religious one, it is not difficult to find excessive devotion to material things. Consider the practice of spending $25,000, $50,000, or more on a Bar or Bat Mitzvah. What is supposed to be a rite of passage for a thirteen-year-old becomes a lavish display of the wealth or social standing of the parents. No matter how flawless the child's Hebrew or how kosher the food, one is still prompted to ask whether the purpose of the event is to honor God or mammon. A similar question can be asked about the practice of putting the names of benefactors on books, chairs, Torah covers, paintings, windows, and practically everything else that goes into a synagogue. Is the money given to promote study and prayer or to call attention to prominent individuals in the community?

But idolatry in modern times is not limited to spending on material things. Newspapers are filled with astrology charts designed to help people predict their future or discover important facts about their character. What purpose does all this serve except to suggest that stars and planets can control the destiny of people on earth? Millions of people, including the most observant Jews, continue to act as if burial places, historic sites, and religious implements have magical powers or provide special access to God. Faith healing is prevalent in nearly every religion and typically works with the same pitch: pay the price, receive the blessing, and wait for the miracle. Religious cults centered around a single individual who speaks for God and directs the course of people's lives are as common today as they ever were. In the debate over gender neutrality, extremists on one side insist that God must be associated with male characteristics, while extremists on the other call on the names of ancient goddesses.

All forms of idolatry have one thing in common: They reject the first and second commandments, which teach that the universe is divided into two mutually exclusive categories—God and everything else. "The heavens," as the Psalmist (115:16) tells us, "are the heavens of the Lord, but the earth has been given to the sons and daughters of humans." Behind this division is a judgment about their status: God is perfect and everlasting; nothing in the created order is. It follows that God cannot be compared to anything in the created order, and nothing in the created order can be treated as divine.

According to Maimonides, the trouble starts when people look for intermediaries who are supposed to have a foot in each realm.[7] Imagine a king who rules over a vast empire. People show respect for the king by respecting his counselors and officers. But, Maimonides continues, it is exactly the opposite with God: People are *not* showing respect for God when they worship the stars, the planets, or the sun; rather they are ignoring God and worshipping surrogates.

Even if we move from the heavens to intermediaries on earth, Maimonides' point is still valid. Whether it is a piece of clay, a religious implement, or a charismatic leader does not matter; monotheism is compromised as soon as people think that a finite object or human being either resembles or functions as a surrogate for God. The next step is to claim that because this person or thing seems to be partly of the divine realm, it too is worthy of worship or adoration. What follows is a series of catastrophic mistakes: If God is holy, a piece of clay shaped in the image of God must be treated with special care; if God is powerful, a religious implement favored by God must be able to ward off disease; if God is all-knowing, the cult leader who speaks for God must be obeyed at any cost. In truth, the piece of clay is an illusion, the religious implement a device for inducing prayer, and the cult leader a human being with an inflated sense of self-worth.

It would be safe to say, then, that the litmus test for being a Jew is seeing things in the created order for what they are: natural objects of finite value and duration. This does not mean that nothing in the created order is worthy of attention or devotion; it means that attention or devotion are one thing, worship and adoration another. To take an obvious example, people from all over the world come to Jerusalem to see the Western Wall; but it is folly to think that by praying there, you are coming face to face with the God of Abraham, Isaac, and Jacob. For all its historical significance, the Wall is a human artifact made from the same kind of materials that went into the construction of the Pyramids, the temples of

Babylon, and the Palace of King Minos. As the Psalmist (96:5) proclaims: all the gods of the nations are vanities. This is as true for the gods themselves as it is for the buildings and artifacts used to serve them. And unless we think about what we are doing, it will be true for our buildings and artifacts as well.

# ▣ The Difficulty of Passing the Test

Idolatry is a complex phenomenon that rears its head in every age. Far from being limited to the worship of clay statues, it provides ample temptation today and is likely to provide temptation tomorrow as well. Anything can become an idol if it comes to be regarded as the be-all and end-all of human life. According to the rabbinic tractate on idolatry (*Avodah Zarah* 54b), philosophers asked the Jews of Rome why an all-powerful God does not abolish idolatry once and for all. The answer was that God would abolish it *if* doing so meant getting rid only of things the world could do without. But since people worship the stars, the planets, the sun, and the moon, God cannot destroy the universe on account of fools.

To this list we can add historic sites, religious implements, attractive men and women, clothes, jewelry, political power, and everything else mentioned in the previous section. As long as there is a created order, someone will be tempted to worship part of it. Even the State of Israel, the various movements within Judaism, and the Jewish people itself (*klal Yisrael*) can become idols if we forget that they are institutions under God whose purpose is to serve God.

If there is more to idolatry than bowing to a piece of clay, there is more to resisting it than routinely celebrating established holidays. No commandment limits the amount of money that can be spent on a Bar or Bat Mitzvah; no prayerbook reminds us that God cannot be found in a wall; no line of Torah prohibits fanatical devotion to a religious leader.

The problem, as Abraham J. Heschel put it, is that monotheism is at variance with powerful human instincts.[8] According to the first and second commandments, the only thing worthy of worship is something we cannot see, touch, build, paint, or imagine—and nothing that we *can* see, touch, build, paint, or imagine can serve as a substitute. This means that even the mightiest forces on earth, the most ferocious animals, the most beautiful objects, or the most powerful potentates are as nothing when compared with God. Isaiah (40:15–18) tells us:

> *Behold, the nations are as a drop of a bucket,*
> *And are counted as the small dust of the balance,*
> *Behold, the isles are as a mote in the weight.*
> *And Lebanon is not sufficient fuel,*
> *Nor the beasts thereof sufficient for burnt-offerings.*

*All the nations are as nothing before Him;*
*They are accounted by Him as things of*
*nought, and vanity.*
*To whom then will you liken God?*
*Or what likeness will you compare unto*
*him?*

The problem is that the nations of the earth, the cedars of Lebanon, the beasts of the field, and the kings who rule over them do not live in heaven; they are real—they occupy space and affect people's lives. The tendency to conceive of God along the lines afforded by people and natural objects runs deep. If God is all-powerful, why should we not take a mighty ruler, a towering mountain, a stately tree, or a vicious beast as an image? And if we do have images, why should we not have a separate god corresponding to each one? In short, what is so important about saying that God is one?

At an elementary level, "God is one" means that there is only one God, not 12, 256, or 728 gods. But mere singularity is not monotheism, and Heschel was right to ask whether singularity alone is worth the price of martyrdom that so many Jews have paid. A person who believes that Baal alone is divine is not a monotheist even if only one god is involved. In fact, "God is one" is not really a numerical claim at all. From an arithmetic standpoint, the difference between one and two is no different than that between any integer and its successor. From a religious standpoint, however, the difference between one and two is all-important, for once we leave unity, we lose any grasp of divinity. We can therefore follow Maimonides in saying that God is not one in the way that a building, an animal, or a book is one: God is not a whole of parts or an item that belongs in a number series.[9]

According to Maimonides, to say that God is one is to say something much more important: that God has no equal, that nothing in the universe can be compared to God or stand as a rival to God. In other words, God is not a bigger, stronger, more formidable version of something found on earth. When the second commandment forbids us from drawing pictures of God, the point is not that you *could* draw one if the prohibition were lifted but that God's perfection cannot be represented in a visual medium. In the early part of the twentieth century Hermann Cohen captured this point by saying that when applied to God, *one* really means *unique*.[10] As we saw above, even the most exalted things on earth are as nought when compared to God. In the words of Isaiah (40:25): "To whom will you liken Me that I should be equal?"[11]

Why is it so difficult to believe in a God who is truly unique? The answer is that if we take uniqueness seriously, there is nothing in human experience that can serve as a model for God—not natural objects and not human images like those of kings, parents, employers, marriage partners, or any of the other comparisons used in the prayerbook. It is true, of course, that God has sovereignty over the world. But divine sovereignty is nothing like human sovereignty. Kings do not create the realm over which they hold sway: They either conquer it or inherit it. By the same token, kings enter into treaties with other kings and live with the possibility that some disgruntled subject will try to overthrow them. What is more, we have seen that showing respect for God is nothing like showing respect for a mortal ruler. So while God is often described as a king, this comparison, like all others, breaks down as soon as we consider its implications.

How, then, do we worship a God who is comparable to nothing? How do we remain true to Isaiah's claim that God has no equal? The hard way is to recognize that human experience is limited and that God transcends everything that can be measured in human terms. Even the wisest person has no idea what it is like to comprehend all truth that ever was or will be in a single moment, and even the most powerful has no idea what it is like to create whole galaxies out of nothing.

Unfortunately, it is difficult to think about divine transcendence and human limits for very long. Sooner or later, we all need a model to help us think about God, and the only place to look for one is our own experience. God is a parent, shepherd, big brother or sister, friend, or teacher. The problem is that once we have a model, we compromise God's uniqueness. Instead of seeing the universe in terms of two categories—God and everything else—we now see it in terms of one category and one mode of experience: our own. In short, once we have a model, we have taken the first step down the road to idolatry.

That is why idolatry is difficult for even the most pious and God-fearing people to avoid. It is difficult to read the prayerbook and realize that all the comparisons used to describe God are inadequate, difficult to visit a historical site such as the Western Wall and remember that God can be found anywhere, difficult to walk into a luxurious synagogue and say to yourself that in principle it is no holier than a log cabin. If idolatry is the litmus test for being a Jew, it is difficult to be a Jew.

It may be the case that if we looked hard enough, we would find that Moses, Isaiah, Rabbi Akiba, Rashi, and Maimonides all had moments of weakness when they thought of God in spatial or anthropomorphic terms. Maybe the first person to pass the test will be the baby crying in the last row of the synagogue. I hope to show here that even if all these suppositions are true, we still have to make the effort. According to the Mishnah, the fact that we cannot complete a task by ourselves does not mean we are free to ignore it.[12] Sometimes progress is made in fractions of inches, sometimes by reviewing a previous advance and preventing a relapse. In either case, we have to put aside pat answers and look at our religion in a critical way.

# Compromising with the Enemy

I have argued that all Judaism rests on insights contained in the first two commandments. It would make my task much easier if I could show that Jewish tradition is single-minded in affirming monotheism and rejecting idolatry, that every line of Torah, every midrash, ritual, prayer, or song is unswerving in its commitment to these ideals. The fact is, however, that the tradition does not always face the enemy and move forward. Sometimes it makes compromises, sometimes it moves laterally, sometimes it appears to take a step backwards.

If you cannot make graven images of God, why are there so many passages in the Bible that encourage you to make mental ones? The opening chapters of Genesis depict God like an ancient king with a heavenly court.[13] We have seen that Noah was supposed to walk with God. Like pagan gods, God works miracles near large bodies of water and makes important speeches from mountain tops. Both Isaiah (6:1–3) and Ezekiel (1:26–29) claim they saw God seated on a throne; in the latter case, the prophet goes so far as to say that God's likeness resembles that of a human being. Throughout midrashic literature, God is depicted as a man on a throne who wears a robe, sheds tears, dons tefillin, and presides over a heavenly court.

Judaism also contains a full range of incarnation metaphors. The Shekhinah, or indwelling presence of God, is said to enter and leave the world, feel pain, dwell among the people, and fill the tent of meeting.[14] There is even a tradition that claims God's Shekhinah, conceived as female, engages in holy intercourse with Moses.[15] To be sure, many of these passages contain the qualifying expression *kivyakhol* (as it were). It is as if

God sheds tears or feels pain. But even with qualifying expressions, literature that depicts God in human form cannot help but raise questions. Why are there so many concessions to anthropomorphism?

Whether we like it or not, the battle against idolatry appears to be fought with two steps forward and one step backward. In this respect, it resembles the story of the Exodus. Rather than describing the choice between monotheism and idolatry philosophically, the Torah represents it geographically. Pharaoh's Egypt is not only the house of bondage but the paradigm of a pagan culture: rich, autocratic, polytheistic, and heavily dependent on magic. By contrast, the Promised Land is a place where free men and women can worship a God who abhors magic, superstition, and extremes of social inequality. Unfortunately the choice between them is not as simple as it appears. From the moment the people are rescued at the Red Sea, they express the desire to return to Egypt and revert to being slaves.[16]

Throughout this study it will become clear that Judaism is a religion of contrasts. In addition to Egypt and the Promised Land, there is heaven and earth, the starkness of the desert and the luxury of the Tabernacle, six days of work and one day of rest, monotheism and paganism, the sacred and the profane. Each of these contrasts presents a tension, and each tension offers the possibility of fudging and backsliding. As we will see, the difficulties of balancing religious demands and human limitations are as real for us as they were for our ancestors. If they traded spiritual growth for material comfort, so do we; if they needed tangible symbols of their commitment to an intangible God, we do as well.

In one respect backsliding is the result of human frailty: Any time a test is difficult to pass, there will be people who think the standards are too high. But in another respect backsliding is indicative of the seriousness of the problem. I have argued that the divine order and the created one are separate, that idolatry occurs when people try to have a leg in each. If so, then we face the question of how the two orders are related. Some religions answer this question by trying to bring God "down to earth." In Christianity, for example, God has a son who takes on characteristics of each realm. Although there are attempts to bring God down to earth in Judaism as well, in general this solution will not work. The question is how we can explain the relation between heaven and earth while preserving the identity of each. How can we set our sights on heaven while keeping in mind that we are only human?

This book will examine these issues and look for answers that reflect the wisdom of a 3,000-year-old tradition. We should keep in mind, however, that if the tensions are real, they can never be completely resolved. We are not spiritual creatures, and it is fruitless to recommend something no one can achieve. The goal, then, is to carry the battle forward and hope that we will be one step closer to the day when we can face the contrasts, raise our level of worship, and resist the temptation to bow to anything but the one true God.

# CHAPTER TWO

# The Idol and Its Allure

For My Thoughts are not your thoughts,
Neither are your ways My ways, saith the Lord.
For as the heavens are higher than the earth,
So are My ways higher than your ways,
And my thoughts than your thoughts.

Isaiah 55:8–9

# ▦ Images of Divinity

According to the second commandment, *any* material representation of God is impermissible; it is just as wrong to portray God as a mighty warrior as it is to portray God as a water nymph. But we need to be more precise on what idolatry is and why it is wrong. Let me therefore propose the following definition: If monotheism is worship of a God who is unique, idolatry is worship of a god who is not unique. If monotheism looks to a God who is beyond heaven and earth, idolatry looks to a god who is part of heaven and earth. We will pursue this contrast on three levels, and at each step it will become clear that idolatry is more than a miscalculation: It is an alluring phenomenon that plays on human vanity.

We can grasp this point by recognizing that the way people depict God says a great deal about the way they conceive God. In Greek mythology, male gods tend to be virile, aggressive, and adept at enforcing their will, while goddesses tend to be voluptuous or athletic.[1] Obviously these images represent fantasies people have about themselves, but at a deeper level they express the values of a culture, in this case a dominant warrior class that favored the athletically gifted over the handicapped, youth over age, power and fertility over intelligence. An idol, then, is more than a harmless representation; since certain values are ascribed to the gods, the idol encourages people to think that those values are ultimate, for example, strength and beauty are so important that we cannot imagine the gods without them.

At a rudimentary level, to say that God cannot be depicted in a material medium is to say that muscles, sex organs, hair color, body type, and facial characteristics have nothing to do with divinity. When the second commandment prohibited image-making, it asked people to abandon the values of a warrior class and look at the world from a new and revolutionary perspective: one that regards moral qualities such as justice and mercy as more important than physical form. In other words, it asked people to look upon physical form, hair color, and body type as vanities that have nothing to do with the value of life. To people who spend thousands of dollars on cosmetics or who rely on steroids or breast implants to provide what nature did not, the lesson is still valid. Let us therefore consider the first level at which idolatry manifests itself: self-love.

## ▣ Idolatry as Narcissism

Imagine that you believed in a god whose likeness could be captured in visual form, a god who resembled human beings in important ways and whose glory could be depicted in stone or on canvas. It does not take much reflection to see that if god looks like us, acts like us, and thinks like us, then in bowing to an image of god, we are really bowing to our own image. We can therefore appreciate the remarks of Xenophanes, a proto-monotheist living in Greece in the sixth century B.C.E., who said that the Ethiopians depict their gods as snub-nosed and black, the Thracians depict theirs as having red hair and blue eyes, and if horses could draw, they would depict theirs with a long mane, four legs, and a tail.

Judaism's response is that we should not even begin to conceive of God in this way. If we could, if we were allowed to represent God in plastic form or to focus our attention on a mental image of God, we would fall into the same trap that captured the Ethiopians and Thracians: we would ascribe to God the qualities we see in ourselves. And when we entered the Holy of Holies expecting to encounter the divine essence, we would be looking at our own.[2]

So strong is the Jewish prohibition against image worship that when the Torah talks about important characters such as Abraham, Sarah, Jacob, and Moses, it provides almost no visual detail. We are never told what kind of clothes they wear or what kind of weapons they carry. In fact, we are not even given basic information such as hair color, skin color, or body weight.

The Torah's silence on these matters stands in marked contrast to the *Iliad,* where Homer goes to great lengths to say how his characters get dressed, what clothing they put on, and how they go into battle. In many instances the visual detail is so rich that it is easy for the reader to get lost in a welter of sights, sounds, smells, and textures. At the end of Book 18, for example, Homer takes nearly 150 lines to describe Achilles' shield. At the end of Book

19 he takes 50 lines to say how the helmets of the Greek soldiers reflect sunlight.

But suppose that someone reading the story of the binding of Isaac asked what Abraham was wearing when he led Isaac to the mountain. The question seems too ridiculous to discuss. We know that Abraham was eager to do God's will even if it meant killing his son; the question of how he looked has no bearing on the story. By the same token, we know that Jacob favored Joseph by giving him a special coat, but we have no idea what color it was or how Joseph looked when he wore it.

The Torah's treatment of its characters is a preparation for its treatment of God. We know that God created heaven and earth, parted the Red Sea, and led the Israelites through the desert. But when Moses asks to see the face of God at Exodus 33:18, he is told that the request is impossible to grant. The problem is not that God is another Medusa, so that any mortal who looks at the divine face will turn to stone, nor that God is like one of the Persian kings who addressed their subjects from behind a curtain. It is that God does not have a face in the literal sense of the term. In fact, God does not have any physical characteristics at all.[3] The expression "face of God" is just a figurative way of talking about being in the presence of God. When the Torah (Exodus 33:11) says that Moses spoke to God "face to face," all it means is that Moses communicated with God directly. As Moses reminds the people at Deuteronomy 4:12, they heard a voice at Sinai but saw no form.

Narcissism is more than a visual phenomenon. Even if one is not so naive as to think that God has two eyes and two ears and looks like a member of the family, it is tempting to think that God resembles us in other respects. Some people think that because God created the world and has sovereignty over it, God must be conceived in masculine terms. Since all nouns in Hebrew are either masculine or feminine, much of the sacred literature of Judaism encourages gender distinctions where none are valid. On the High Holy Days, for example, we pray to *Avinu Malkenu* (our Father, Our King). But there is nothing sacrosanct about male sex organs, behavior patterns, or social roles.[4]

By the same token, there is nothing sacrosanct about female alternatives. Some people have argued that the best way to counteract centuries of male domination is to introduce modern forms of goddess worship. Instead of correcting the problem, however, this suggestion only compounds it. To claim that God is male or female, black or white, young or old, is to glorify a stereotype. At bottom, it is no better than claiming that God must have red hair or a snub nose. Once we identify God with any portion of the human race, we raise the question of what to do with the rest. If God is black, what does that imply about whites? If God is male, what does that imply about females? In fact, God is "none of the above," and the importance of this fact is that everyone can be considered a creature of God.

But narcissism involves more than race or gender. It is tempting for men and women to think that God likes what they like, shares their view of current events, prefers their way of life to all others, and contemplates the universe from their perspective. All these attitudes are ways of projecting our image onto God, of thinking that heaven and earth revolve around us. At its core, idolatry is a form of flattery, and this fact explains its appeal to the human psyche, its appeal throughout history, and its appeal today. It is comforting to think that God looks like you rather than your enemies, that God inhabits your territory and stands for your ideas.

Rather than to glorify our biases or convictions, the purpose of monotheistic religion is to do the opposite: induce a feeling of awe and humility in the presence of One infinitely greater than us. Monotheism therefore demands that when we enter the Holy of Holies, we take a critical attitude toward human accomplishments, seeing them as neither ultimate nor irreplaceable. That is why Isaiah tells us that God does not think human thoughts and cannot be described in human terms. It is also why the Torah (Deuteronomy 10:18) claims that God loves the stranger, the non-Jew, the person who may not look like you, believe what you believe, or act the way you act. At a minimal level, to think like a monotheist is to give up any form of cultural or religious chauvinism.

# Idolatry as Magic

Not all cultures worshipped their gods in human form. Does the worship of trees, animals, natural forces such as lightning or thunder, and heavenly bodies falls outside the scope of what Judaism terms idolatry? Of course not. If we are to understand idolatry in all its forms, we have to broaden the scope of the argument. Idolatry includes *any* portrayal of God as *any* material thing, force, or being.

Why do we need so expansive a definition? Because everything material is finite, whereas God is not. Whether we are dealing with skyscrapers, oceans, or galaxies, every material object has a limit to its strength or influence. By the same token, every material force can be blunted by another force. Raging storms dissipate when wind currents shift, volcanoes become inactive when the earth below them settles, and even the sun will burn itself out over time. To conceive of God in material terms is to limit God, and a limited conception of God leads directly to the trap of thinking that we or some superior power can control God.

Again, we can understand the problem by looking to mythology. Poseidon, the god of the sea, presented a formidable obstacle to sailors but had to bow to the power of Zeus. Zeus, in turn, ruled over all the gods and goddesses on Mount Olympus but had to bow to the power of the Fates. But even the Fates were not ultimate. Legend has it that Apollo rendered them helpless by getting them drunk. Each time we identify a finite power, we raise the possibility of finding a superior one. If a superior one exists, the first can be controlled or manipulated by an appeal to the second.

What do power, limits on power, and the human

wish to control one power by appealing to another have to do with idolatry? The Torah often connects idolatry with magic. At Deuteronomy 18:9–12, for example, God forbids any Israelite from being a soothsayer, augurer, sorcerer, charmer, wizard, medium, or necromancer. In short, the passage prohibits anyone from looking for forces with which to manipulate God. The biblical historian Yehezkel Kaufmann notes that pagan cultures in the ancient Near East typically thought of their gods as either practicing magic or falling victim to it.[5] We have seen that the archetype of all pagan cultures is Egypt. According to Nahum Sarna:

> *Egypt, especially, was the classic land of magic, which played a central role in its religious life. In fact, magic permeated every aspect of life. The number of gods in Egypt was almost unlimited. One version of the Book of the Dead mentions over five hundred. This prodigious multiplicity of divine beings in itself meant that no god could be either infinite or absolute. Moreover, the inherence of the gods in nature, their dependence upon the physical and the material for their continued existence, further limited their scope. They, like human beings, were deemed to be subject to superior forces inherent in the primordial realm of existence, a meta-divine realm from which the gods themselves derive. Human destiny was thought to be controlled*

*by two distinct forces, the gods and the powers beyond the gods. Neither of these was necessarily benevolent. In fact, antagonism and malevolence were considered to be characteristic of the divine relationship with man. Inevitably, religion became increasingly concerned with the elaboration of ritual designed to propitiate or neutralize the numerous unpredictable powers that be. Man had to be able to devise the means whereby those powers inherent in the meta-divine realm could be activated for his benefit. Magic thus became an integral part of religion. Even the gods were believed to resort to magic against one another.[6]*

Strange as this worldview may seem, it has one great selling point: it raises the possibility that we can find something that will do for us what alcohol did for Apollo, that we can make the rain come or the sun shine by saying the right words, wearing the right clothes, or dancing the right dance.

It is hardly surprising, then, that pagan religions were full of magical chants, spells, charms, amulets, healing devices, special foods, lucky and unlucky days, magical numbers, and a vast array of secret rituals. And since the ancient Israelites were not immune to the desire to control God, neither is it surprising that many of them trusted magic despite repeated attempts to proclaim it a sham.[7] The Bible (I Samuel 4:3) tells us, for example, that people believed that if they went into battle with the Ark of the Covenant, they would emerge victorious. Throughout the ages, Jewish folklore has been full of jinxes, curses, demons, amulets, magical names, magical numbers, and other forms of superstition.[8] Here again the lure of idolatry has nothing to do with national boundaries.

But my interest is more in law than in folklore. Are there not special foods, special clothes, sacred chants, and special rituals in Judaism as well? Are they not important parts of our understanding of spirituality?

Although the answer to both questions is yes, the single most important contribution of Judaism to world culture is that, when it is properly understood, no article or ritual has any magical power. Lighting candles on Shabbat will not ensure a prosperous week, eating matzah on Passover will not improve one's health, wearing a yarmulke will not ward off evil spirits, putting a mezuzah on the doorpost of one's house will have no effect on floods, fire, theft, or vandalism. Rather than good luck charms, these implements serve as symbols or reminders: Shabbat candles of creation, matzah of the Exodus from Egypt, a mezuzah that Israel is a people in convenant with God. Apart from their educational function, the candles are just pieces of wax, the matzah a sheet of bread, and the mezuzah a piece of parchment.

The problem is that it is difficult to use them without believing that they do have special powers. There is always a temptation to think that if we observe the rituals closely enough, we can force God to show some favor or grant some wish. This is the same temptation that led our ancestors to kneel before statues, put their children through fires, and build shrines on mountaintops. In our day it is even possible to Fax prayers to God by calling a service in Israel that puts the prayers on little sheets of paper and deposits them in cracks in the Western Wall. Tefillin blessed by a particular rabbi are sold to people in hospitals, and cemetery plots near historical sites fetch huge sums of money. In less extreme cases, people believe that by obeying rituals, they are somehow putting God in their debt. Perhaps it is difficult *not* to believe this if you are suffering from an illness, embarking on a dangerous mission, or trying to recover from a personal tragedy. At times everyone feels that events in his or her life are out of control and that fortune has put too many obstacles in the way of happiness. Idolatry offers the illusion that by joining a cult or following a closely defined set of rules, one can regain control.

The illusion is very appealing. Our ancestors turned to the Golden Calf after Moses left them alone in the desert for 40 days. Although we normally look upon this episode as one of the worst in Jewish history, we must ask whether our responses in moments of crisis are any better. If we turn to the occult, or try to endow sacred rituals with magical significance, they are not. The person who enters a sanctuary expecting to gain an advantage over disease, famine, unemployment, or unpopularity is committing the same sin all over again.

There is, of course, an obvious objection to what I have said: What about the efficacy of prayer? Does Judaism not encourage people to pray for peace, health, prosperity, mutual understanding, and the coming of a messianic age? If these prayers are not effective, why permit them? Why not ask people to bear their troubles in silence?

To answer these questions, we should recognize that not all prayers ask for divine intercession: some praise God, some recall events of the past, some express the human yearning to live in accord with God, and some call upon God to forgive our sins. Even those that do ask for divine intercession try to resist the tendency to regard prayer as a way of enhancing personal power. Thus all prayers, whether implicitly or explicitly, take the following form: *Y'hi ratzon Adonai Elohenu* (May it be thy will, O Lord our God . . .). The person who beseeches God in this manner admits that God's will is ultimate. Since God is the creator of everything in heaven or earth, there is no magical power to which God must yield, hence no possibility of pressuring God to do anything. Clearly there is a world of difference between *asking* for peace or health and thinking one can *force* or *trick* God into delivering it. According to Kaufmann, the characteristic feature of pagan religion is that ritual is thought to be automatically effective.[9] It made no difference whether a person was selfish or charitable, honest or hypocritical: ritual was supposed to bring the desired result no matter who used it or for what purpose.

The folly of idolatry is that we can never be in a position to exert pressure on God or to make God respond to us as a genie in a bottle would. We can ask for something, but the decision to grant our request is one that God makes without compulsion. This is another way of saying that nothing can control the will of God save God. To the degree that magic encourages us to think we can interfere with God's will, it, like narcissism, is a form of flattery.

# ▣ Philosophy as Idolatry

Throughout this chapter I have argued that God does not resemble an animal, a material object, a material force, a person, or a heavenly body. To the question, "What does God resemble?" the only valid reply is: nothing. As we have seen, next to God, everything else in the universe counts for naught. If this is true, then how can a fallible creature conceive of God? Our language, thought, and scientific theories are designed to deal with ordinary objects: plants, animals, people, material forces, and the like. If God does not resemble any of these things, how can we hope to understand God? How can we find the terms to describe something that is utterly unique? For each time we compare God to something in our experience, we will defeat our purpose.

To see the problem in another light, consider the following dilemma. Knowledge often implies control.

Hundreds of years ago electricity was considered a strange and unpredictable force; now that we have a better understanding of it, we can generate it, store it, transmit it, and turn it on or off at will. The result is that electricity has become a normal part of our lives. In this day and age no one is thrilled by turning on a light switch or amazed at the phenomenon of recorded sound.

If the same is true of God, the more we know about God, the more mundane God will seem. If God can be described in terms that apply to ordinary objects, our idea of God will resemble our idea of ourselves, and once again we will fall prey to idolatry. By contrast, the more we emphasize God's uniqueness, the less we will be able to know about God. Unlike electricity, God will fit no category and fall under no scientific law. It follows that no matter how we think of God, we face a trade-off between uniqueness and intelligibility: emphasize one and we compromise the other.

The traditional Jewish response is to come down on the side of uniqueness. According to Maimonides, all attempts to grasp the essence of God are bound to fail.[10] We can better understand his position by returning to Exodus 33. Moses' request to see the face of God represents the human desire to know God in every detail. When God says that the request cannot be granted, the point is that a part of God will always be shrouded in mystery. We can see the world God created and make an effort to obey the commandments God handed down, but the inner workings of the creator, the essence of God, will always be beyond our ken. If Moses could not see God up close but had to hide in a rock, how much more removed are we? It could be said, therefore, that faced with the trade-off between uniqueness and intelligibility, Maimonides sacrifices intelligibility. In his words, the purpose of the sacred books is not to prevent us from knowing the things science can describe but "to make it known that the intellects of human beings have a limit at which they stop."[11] That limit occurs when we stop talking about the world and start talking about the essence of the One who created it.

Once we have a limit, it is hard not to ask what lies beyond it. What if you could stand with Moses in the rock and steal a glimpse of the forbidden sight? What if you did apply human categories to the divine essence? Tempting as these thoughts are, Maimonides argues that we have to resist them. To push human knowledge beyond its limit is not a way of inching closer to God but a way of inviting arbitrariness and incoherence.

There is a long tradition of philosophers who think that God can be understood scientifically, that the categories and assumptions that explain the natural world can be applied to God. But if God is truly unique, this kind of philosophy is impossible. God cannot be understood scientifically because science is limited to things that can be seen, touched, or measured by human observers. Any attempt to understand God scientifically is an attempt to pierce the veil of mystery and do what even Moses could not. In sum, uncritical philosophy opts for the other side of the dilemma: faced with a trade-off between uniqueness and intelligibility, it tries to come down on the side of intelligibility.

To the degree that philosophy sacrifices God's uniqueness, we must ask whether it too represents a form of
idolatry. Is it not presumptuous to think that the human
mind can investigate the inner reaches of God? Can we
possibly understand the workings and motivations of
God? If the answer is no, then this kind of philosophy can
also be a form of flattery, a way of making us think we
are better than we are. This is not to say that all philosophy is illegitimate. We can imagine a theory that takes
cognizance of God's uniqueness by stressing the fallibility
of human knowledge rather than the breadth of its reach.
It would highlight the wisdom that comes with admitting
there are questions to which we do not and will never know
the answer. In short, it would be a critique of human
knowledge rather than an attempt to extend knowledge
into ever more speculative realms. As Maimonides put
it: "Glory then to Him who is such that when the intellects contemplate His essence, their apprehension turns
to incapacity; and when they contemplate the proceed-
ing of His actions from His will, their knowledge turns
into ignorance; and when the tongues aspire to magnify
Him by means of attributive qualifications, all eloquence
turns into weariness and incapacity!"[12]

To borrow a phrase from the late medieval philosopher Nicholas of Cusa, this sort of philosophy would
be a form of "learned ignorance." Each time we felt we
had unlocked the mysteries of the universe and come to
see what God is, we would remind ourselves that once
we leave the realm of things we can see, touch, or measure, what we call knowledge is in fact guesswork. I

mention philosophy because it is a mistake to think that idolatry presents a problem only for the uneducated. If idolatry is worship of a god who is not unique, it is just as easy to succumb to it at an advanced level as it is at an elementary one. From a religious point of view, reason is not a panacea. On the contrary, reason that does not recognize its limits, that operates on the assumption that everything can be explained by the categories we devise, is as much a threat to monotheism as drawing pictures of God. The inescapable conclusion is that the allure of idolatry is universal, affecting moderns as well as ancients, great thinkers as well as ordinary people.

## "I am the first, and I am the last . . . "

Let us now take stock. Idolatry is not an isolated act but rather a comprehensive worldview according to which nothing is unique and everything can be measured or conceived in human terms. The purpose of Judaism or any monotheistic religion is to persuade people to abandon this worldview and adopt one in which humans are not the measure of all things but are created by and ruled over by God. According to Isaiah:

> *I am the first, and I am the last,*
> *And besides Me there is no God. (44:6)*

By "God" he means something of ultimate value, something that *is* worthy of worship or adoration. God, in turn, cannot be seen, controlled, or completely understood. To believe in God is to stand in awe of something that is not only greater than you but greater than anything you can imagine.

If this view of God is on the right track, then like many conceptual advances, it answers one set of questions only to raise another. If emphasizing God's infinite superiority allows us to expose human vanity, it calls into question the relation between God and humans. How can a God who is utterly unique be accessible to people who are not? How can we pay homage to a God who is beyond our comprehension? How can the idea of uniqueness be made concrete? Would a certain amount of backsliding not be desirable? It is to these questions that we now turn.

# CHAPTER THREE

# Sacred Space

And let them make me a sanctuary,
that I may dwell among them.

Exodus 25:8

# ▦ Monotheism
# Made Concrete

Since monotheism is founded on the idea that the universe is divided into two realms, we face an obvious problem. We live in the created order. Since nothing in our experience resembles God, how can we have a religion whose purpose is to worship God? How do you encourage people in one realm to bow their heads to something in the other? Or, to put the question a different way, what is to prevent the two realms from becoming so separate that we forget about God altogether? Since the created order can be viewed either spatially or temporally, it would be helpful to raise these questions from each perspective. Can a certain part of space or a particular stretch of time be sacred? Does the idea of sacred space or time compromise monotheism? This chapter will take up the issue of space and the next one will deal with time.

First a word of explanation. By *sacred space* I do not mean that something in the created order can become a vessel *for* God, but rather that something has been identified as a place where people can express their devotion *to* God. The need for such space is clear. Uniqueness, transcendence, and divinity are abstract ideas. It is all very well to say that people should acknowledge God's uniqueness, but it is impossible for anyone to exist on a diet of abstraction alone. From time to time we all need tangible symbols such as artwork, jewelry, special clothing, monuments, or official residences to remind us of the values we stand for.

We can appreciate the need for symbolism by looking at a secular idea, such as democracy. At an elementary level, democracy means that every citizen has a right to vote. But if we take America as a model, democracy also involves free speech, equal protection under the law, and separation of church and state. In their own way, these ideas are as abstract as uniqueness and transcendence. If people are to accept democracy and even risk their lives to defend it, they need symbols such as the White House, the flag, or the Statue of Liberty. On a smaller scale, branches of the armed services have their own insignia, universities their caps and gowns, athletic teams their mascots, and corporations their logos.

The problem is that once tangible symbols are developed and begin to attract loyalty, people may pay more attention to the symbol than they do to the reality; in a religious context, they may begin to worship the symbol and forget about God. Another problem is that people may come to regard the symbol as part of God or a vessel in which God is housed. Even if these traps are avoided, there is always the possibility that someone will imbue the symbol with magical significance, thinking that it can ward off disease or guarantee happiness. In short, in any religion there is a fine line between the rarefied air of theological abstraction and the concrete world of cups, candle holders, ark covers, priestly vestments, and luxurious sanctuaries. With this type of problem, there is no simple formula for deciding where the line should be drawn. Some worshippers need pictures on every wall while others prefer more spartan surroundings. In either case, the question is how to prevent symbols from becoming surrogates.

The Torah addresses this issue when God asks the people to build a Tabernacle (Exodus 25–30; 35–40). It is difficult to read the description of the Tabernacle, its furniture, and the priestly vestments without feeling a certain amount of unease. We saw in the previous chapter that the Torah contains very little visual detail. When we get to Exodus 25, however, the visual detail becomes just as rich as Homer's. There are constant references to gold, silver, and precious stones; frequent mention of cherubim; elaborate designs for robes, hats, and rings; as well as a detailed account of how everything is to be made. Unlike other parts of the Torah, this one practically begs us to let our imaginations run wild. We must therefore ask why an important symbol of monotheism sounds as if it belongs in a pagan culture.

# ▣ Worshipping God in Luxury

The Tabernacle was a rectangular structure 100 cubits long and 50 cubits wide.[1] It was constructed of wooden poles and enclosed in a fabric made of fine linen with blue, purple, and scarlet threads. The structure was subdivided into two squares 50 cubits on a side. The first square was the Outer Court and contained a laver and an altar for burnt offerings. The first part of the second square was an area known as the Holy Place and contained an altar for burning incense, a table for displaying bread, and a lamp stand. Beyond the Holy Place was the Holy of Holies, a veiled area 10 cubits on a side, housing the Ark of the Covenant.

In brief, the Ark was a wooden chest designed to house the tablets of the law. The Ark, table, and altar were all acacia wood overlaid with gold. The lamp stand, pans, jars, and bowls were pure gold. The tabernacle was covered with animals skins and the various sections divided by elaborately decorated curtains. Even more elaborate were the priestly vestments, which were made of gold, brightly colored linen, and precious stones.

Scholars have long questioned how a band of slaves wandering in the desert could come up with enough gold, silver, precious stones, fine linen, goatskins, sealskins, dyes, tools, and acacia wood to undertake such a project.[2] By one estimate, the Tabernacle would have contained one ton of gold, three tons of silver, and two and a half tons of bronze.[3] Even if such materials were available, it is hard to see how they could have been carried from place to place. Still, the real question raised by the Tabernacle is not technical but religious: Why do a people who worship a God who cannot be seen *need* such a dazzling spectacle? Why should God not be worshipped in more modest surroundings?

The question of surroundings is not trivial. Pagan shrines were often elaborate structures decorated with vast amounts of gold, jewelry, and meticulously designed works of art. One might expect a monotheistic religion to insist on a very different environment. After all, gold is nothing but an inert metal carrying a high price tag. There is no inherent reason why gold should be favored by God or induce the love of God in us. In a religion founded on magic and superstition, there might be grounds for making implements out of precious materials: people are awed by the sight of enormous wealth. Crowds line up to gaze at the Hope Diamond and the Crown Jewels. Thus one way to grab people's attention and convey the idea that religious observance leads to material prosperity is to make a house of worship look like a jewelry store. But why should a religion that renounces superstition do likewise? Why should a monotheist not be content to worship God in a log cabin?

Even looking beyond the question of surroundings, we might ask a similar question about the articles and implements of prayer. Why do we need richly decorated Torah covers, sterling silver kiddush cups, or ornately designed seder plates? Why not proclaim the glory of God with objects that do not call attention to themselves?

# Sacred and Profane Space

Certainly the Tabernacle is luxurious. But even though its opulence calls to mind a pagan shrine, there are several respects in which it constituted a departure from the religious practices in the Ancient Near East. In the first place, it is not the personal dwelling place of God. The text of Exodus 25:8 says explicitly: "Let them make Me a sanctuary that I may dwell among *them*," not "that I may dwell in *it*." It is not the gold, rare stones, and fine linen that are holy but the services that people perform with them. In other words, the Tabernacle is a place where the people can experience the living presence of God; without this experience, it is just a big tent filled with expensive furniture.[4]

It is also important to recognize that the Tabernacle was a portable structure. When the people assembled it at a certain place, that place became holy. But once the people moved on, the location went back to being an ordinary stretch of desert terrain. For all its splendor, the Tabernacle did not confer any magical power on the ground on which it was located. In this respect, it is like the Burning Bush or Mount Sinai. God picks a spot in the wilderness to talk to Moses, but once the conversation is over, the spot becomes as anonymous as any other.

In fact, portability is an important part of the narrative of the Torah. Pagan gods were often identified with a specific function or location. In Greek mythology, Zeus ruled over the heavens, Poseidon over the sea, and Hades over the underworld. By the same token, Artemis is often associated with forests, Athena with cities, and Demeter with farms. Furthermore, nearly every river or hilltop was supposed to have a god or nymph who watched over it. The result was that if you traveled from one location to another, you could expect to encounter any number of local deities. One of the remarkable features of the Exodus is that change of location has no theological significance: the God who brings the plagues on Egypt is the same as the God who speaks to Moses in the wilderness and helps the people enter the Promised Land. If God is not restricted to a particular location, neither is the Tabernacle. In principle, it could be moved anywhere the people go.

A second feature is that the Tabernacle is not a piece of representational art. Even though it allows God to dwell among the people, it bears no physical resemblance to God, heavenly bodies, natural forces, or wild animals. The Ark, table, and lamp stand are beautifully worked and heavily gilded, but they are not made in the likeness of anything. A person walking through the Tabernacle would not be able to draw any inference about God's face or form.

The chief exception to the rule of representational art is the cherubim depicted on either side of the Ark and throughout much of the rest of the structure. Thus Exodus 25:20: "And the cherubim shall spread out their wings on high, screening the Ark cover with their wings, with their faces one to another."[5] Although we cannot be sure what these creatures looked like or what significance they had, this much is clear: They were purely imaginary. There is no evidence to indicate that they resembled any creature on earth, in the skies, or under the sea. According to Sarna: "They are brilliant, if fantastic, fabrications of the fertile human imagination struggling to express symbolically profound and mystical abstractions."[6] What is more, the cherubim were not objects of worship. Though they are depicted in the Tabernacle, no prayer is directed to them and no offering is made on their behalf; their function appears to be purely decorative.

Finally, it is worth noting how the gold and jewels for the Tabernacle were collected. At Exodus 25:2, God tells Moses to go to the people and ask for gifts to begin work. The picture that emerges stands in sharp contrast to the many passages where the people protest lack of food and water and ask to be taken back to Egypt:

> *And all the congregation of the children of Israel departed from the presence of Moses. And they came, every one whose heart stirred him up, and everyone whom his spirit made willing, and brought the Lord's offering, for the work of the tent of meeting, and for all the service thereof, and for the holy garments. And they came, both men and women, as many as were willing-hearted, and brought nose-rings, and ear-rings, and signet-rings, and girdles, all jewels of gold; even every man that brought an offering of gold unto the Lord. And every man, with whom was found blue, and purple, and scarlet, and fine linen, and goats' hair, and rams' skins dyed red, and seal-skins, brought them. Every one that did set apart an offering of silver and brass brought the Lord's offering; and every man with whom was found acacia wood for any work of the service brought it And all the women*

> *that were wise-hearted did spin with their*
> *hands and brought that which they had*
> *spun, the blue, and the purple, the scarlet,*
> *and the fine linen. And all the women whose*
> *heart stirred them up in wisdom spun the*
> *goats' hair. And the rulers brought the onyx*
> *stones, and the stones to be set, for the*
> *ephod, and for the breastplate; and the*
> *spice, and the oil, for the lighter, and for the*
> *anointing oil, and for the sweet incense.*
> *(Exodus 35:20–28)*

In fact, the people's generosity is so great that by Exodus 36:5, more than enough material has been collected.

Clearly the Tabernacle was a stunning sight. But a number of steps were taken to ensure that the people did not forget the religious principles on which it was founded. Unlike the stone tablets for the Ten Commandments, the Tabernacle was not produced by a miracle. According to Exodus 39:42: "The children of Israel did all the work." It was a community effort: Presumably, the jewelry was melted down and recast, so it would have been impossible to tell who gave the gold for the lamp stand, the Ark, or the table. There are no statues of national heroes, parts of dead bodies, or displays of weapons. Other than stones to represent each tribe, there is nothing that calls attention to particular people. The services conducted in the Tabernacle allowed Moses and the priests to do three things: (1) receive divine revelations, (2) celebrate Shabbat and required festivals, and (3) atone for sin. There was no attempt to communicate with the dead, consecrate sexual activity, or worship ancestors. What is more, all the construction had to stop on Shabbat so that the people, their servants, and beasts of burden could rest.

We can imagine a religion completely devoid of art, but it would be so barren that only an extraordinary person could be drawn to it. So while it may be possible in principle to worship God in a log cabin, for most people it is not possible in fact. At its best, art does what no lecture on theology can: It induces a feeling of reverence for an object in front of you. Who has not walked up to a famous painting and had the feeling, like Moses at the Burning Bush, of treading on sacred ground? I use the term *reverence* because the way we describe art is very close to the way we describe God. Art can be uplifting, revelatory, even awe-inspiring. Sometimes a great work of art is so moving that it makes people reexamine the meaning of their lives, sometimes it leaves them speechless.

It is hardly surprising that the distinction between the sacred and the profane is connected with a parallel distinction between refinement and vulgarity. We expect a house of worship to be a special place that stands apart from ordinary buildings, and we expect people who enter it to show respect. Religion asks us to cleanse our bodies as well as our souls. For Judaism in particular, foods, clothes, or bodily activities that are unclean have no place in a sanctuary. Ritual, then, is not just a way of serving God but a way of elevating ourselves. That is why special care must be taken to ensure that the environment

inspires the right feelings and promotes the proper attitude. Even in the secular realm, refinement is closely connected with dignity or status. We do not expect the
President to live in a shabby house or the Queen to ride
through town on a bicycle.

For the same reason, we do not expect the most important part of the Tabernacle, the Ark of the Covenant,
to be encrusted with tin. There is a natural tendency to
think that the implements of worship should be precious, not because they have to possess great market
value, but because they ought to represent the best work
of which we are capable. The Ark would not command
people's attention or inspire awe if it were thrown together
overnight. Thus Exodus 35:31 tells us that the artist
Bezalel was infused with the spirit of God. This statement can mean only that he was able to make things
that were powerful inducements to worship, so that without him worship would have suffered. If worship suffered,
then no matter how important monotheism is from a
philosophic perspective, it could easily die of neglect.

# ▣ Weaning the People from Idolatry

Once again we face the problem of how and when
to compromise. To the degree that art inspires awe, it can
direct attention away from transitory matters and help

focus it on eternal ones. But to the degree that art inspires awe, it can also become a rival to God. If people were asked whether the Ark *is* God, no one would have said yes. On the other hand, the Ark has one advantage God does not: People can see it. No one requires proof or exhortations to believe that a gold-encrusted chest is real, but people require all manner of proofs and exhortations to believe in God. To return to Maimonides' example from Chapter 1, we can show respect for a mortal king by respecting his intermediaries. For many people, there is a powerful temptation to regard works of art as intermediaries and forget about God altogether.

The problem with intermediaries, then, is that they become objects of worship in their own right. As Solomon Schechter put it, establishing an intermediary between God and humans is tantamount to setting up another God, which is always the cause of sin.[7] This is particularly true if the intermediary is a physical object such as a building or a piece of furniture.

In our time, the Ark of the Covenant has been replaced by the Torah scroll as the center of attention. In principle, the Torah is the written word of God, a body of instruction for all times. But the Torah is also a physical object that we dress in luxury, hold up in the air, kiss, touch, and bow to. Unless we remind ourselves that the Torah is supposed to teach us something, there is a danger that it too might become an idol. We must therefore be on our guard lest Judaism become Torah fetishism. Touching the Torah will not improve your health, and hearing someone read from it will not improve your mind unless you make the effort to understand what is being said. Unfortunately, the Torah is written in a language many Jews do not understand, and public reading of it has become highly ritualized. Rather than a study session, we get a ceremony; rather than instruction, which is the real meaning of the word *torah,* we get spectacle.

Maimonides explains this temptation by saying that people have a love for and inclination to things to which they are accustomed.[8] It is easier to picture an object covered in velvet and dressed with silver than it is to deal with the metaphysical problems of defining a perfect being. Part of the appeal of idolatry is that it ignores these problems and focuses on things we can put in our hands.

If Maimonides is right, if people are naturally disposed to put more emphasis on material things than spiritual matters, then the problem of compromise becomes paramount. Take ark covers, Torah scrolls, name plates, and kiddush cups out of Judaism and idolatry would seem so appealing that no one but a Maimonides could resist it. So even if works of art become distractions, even if people pay so much attention to decoration that they forget about God altogether, we must ask whether it is better to succumb to Torah fetishism than to kneel to a statue of a powerful man or voluptuous woman in modern attire. Obviously, neither alternative is perfect. But if Maimonides' assessment of the human situation is right, is it not better to kneel to a scroll than to a likeness of a person?

The answer is yes, and for many people that is the end of the matter. If idolatry is inevitable, better that we have a diluted version than the full-strength alternative. Still, we can hope that idolatry is not inevitable and that a more suitable compromise is available. On this issue, Maimonides argues that the choice between monotheism and idolatry does not have to be a take-it-or-leave-it proposition: It is possible to wean people away from idolatry in stages.[9] To understand his argument, let us return to the design for the Tabernacle.

According to a tradition that begins with Joshua (24: 14), the Israelites adopted the religious practices of their captors during the Egyptian captivity. Let us therefore imagine a people who have been exposed to monotheism but who find themselves living in a pagan land with luxurious temples, shrines, and mausoleums. Since they are only human, they cannot help but be dazzled by what they see. And since they have no center of worship for their own religion, it is understandable why many would be attracted to paganism.

Now suppose that the people are set free and allowed to worship God in their own way. A typical response would be to build a temple to their God as luxurious as the ones they saw in Egypt. If someone were to say that luxurious surroundings are not necessary to serve God, that God should not be conceived in spatial terms, and that no physical structure can contain God, the people would shake their heads in disbelief. They would be too accustomed to pagan religion to accept monotheism in its pure form.

What would be needed is a transitional device, something that calls to mind the splendor of a pagan shrine but attempts to avoid the most objectionable features. Recall that despite its opulence, the Tabernacle represents a step in the right direction: there are no tombs containing dead bodies and no representational art. The Tabernacle is therefore a symbol with one foot in the old world and one foot in the new. From a literary perspective, it is significant that the description of the Tabernacle occurs in two stages: from Exodus 25 to 31, and from Exodus 35 to 40. Between these passages, two events take place: the Israelites worship the Golden Calf, and the goodness of God is revealed to Moses. The spacing is not accidental. Both the Tabernacle and the Golden Calf are religious symbols made from precious materials. Both satisfy the need to focus on something material. It is true, of course, that one is a permissible form of artistic expression while the other is not, but in contrast to both, the goodness of God is revealed to Moses without any ornaments or symbols at all.

In short, the Tabernacle is a transitional structure that made numerous concessions to human fallibility. It takes the energy that went into the making of an idol and redirects it to a legitimate form of worship; it offers the people a spectacle but stops short of giving them a shrine. It is built on the assumption that physical beauty can be appreciated without becoming an end in itself, that the soul can be inspired to move from a preoccupation with material things to a quest for the spiritual. The Tabernacle is therefore built on the hope that the natural inclination toward material things can be overcome if the transition to the spiritual is smooth enough.

Important as it is, the Tabernacle is not the ultimate expression of Jewish spirituality. We saw that the plan consists of a series of courts and chambers arranged in ascending order of holiness, with the innermost court or Holy of Holies housing the Ark. The closer one gets to the Ark, the more precious the materials become. At Exodus 25:22 we learn that the voice of God will come to Moses from the space on the Ark between the two cherubim — as if God needs a sound system to communicate with people. Clearly this is a step backward. You do not have to imagine yourself in the Holy of Holies to feel that you are in the presence of God. According to *Pirke Avot* (3.3), if two people sit together and discuss the Torah, the Divine presence abides between them — if even one person studies the Torah, God takes notice and appoints a reward. To be sure, the rabbis said this because the Temple in Jerusalem had been destroyed, but whatever the context of the remark, it is a proper expression of a monotheistic religion.

# 🔲 Spectacle and Spirit

Although the Tabernacle is no longer an issue for us, the problem posed by religious art is. We do not have a high priest put on vestments and enter the Holy of Holies, but we do have buildings where heavily decorated Torah scrolls are taken out of the Ark and paraded through the congregation. How do we determine when gold, silver, and ornamentation no longer facilitate worship but detract from it?

It is impossible to answer this question in a simple way because Judaism is not a simple phenomenon. The same generation that built the Tabernacle also built the Golden Calf. In latter ages Jews worshipped God in everything from austere caves to the splendor of Solomon's Temple, from the Dura Europas Synagogue, which made extensive use of representational art borrowed from Greek mythology, to the Transito Synagogue, which contained no representational art at all. It is, of course, forbidden to make images of God. For traditional Jews this prohibition extends to angels, other heavenly creatures, and three-dimensional representations of a complete human body.[10] There are, however, no limits to purely decorative designs such as swirls or geometric figures; they can be as ornate or luxurious as one likes. Again there is a thin line, however: Where does beauty end and extravagance begin?

To answer this question, let me propose the following test. The next time you attend a service, wait 24 hours and ask yourself what you remember most: the physical beauty of the sanctuary; the identity of the people who paid for it; the pomp and circumstance associated with reading the Torah; the robes, gowns, and implements of worship; or the opportunity to study and reflect on a sacred teaching. If the element of reflection is secondary, or if the sights and sounds of the service are so striking that there is no room for reflection at all, something is wrong: too much has been compromised and the process of weaning the people away from idolatry is incomplete.

Although we have focused here on the Tabernacle, it is important to recognize that *any* material thing that attracts us to worship poses the same problem. If the Tabernacle was not intended to be the ultimate expression of Jewish spirituality, neither are the implements with which we decorate our homes or synagogues; if the Tabernacle was a hybrid structure containing elements of both paganism and monotheism, so are modern houses of worship. Their purpose is to take people with a strong predilection for material things and persuade them to devote their lives to the spiritual. They allow people to show that Jewish houses of worship can be as magnificent as those of gentiles. They provide a central location for services, classes, celebrations, and community activities. But in the end, they too run the risk of getting people to think of religion in spatial terms. According to Jewish law, a service can be held wherever ten people gather to pray. If the Tabernacle was a concession to human fallibility, it is unrealistic to expect our buildings to be anything else. The goal is to see concessions for what they are and to work toward something better. In sum, the perfect house of worship has yet to be built.

CHAPTER FOUR

# Sacred Time

The children of Israel shall
keep the Sabbath and observe
the Sabbath throughout all
generations, for a perpetual
covenant. It is a sign between
Me and the children of Israel
forever. . . .

Exodus 31:16–17

# ▣ Service to Strange Gods

Now that we have looked at sacred space, let us consider sacred time. How should time be structured to allow God to play an important role in our lives? How can people who need to earn a living, run a house, and participate in family life take time to think about uniqueness and transcendence? Does the Torah make compromises here too? In thinking about time, it is well to remember that according to the second commandment, it is not just bowing to idols that is objectionable but bowing and *serving*. In fact, the rabbinic term for idolatry (*avodah zarah*) means "strange service." So in addition to thinking about idolatry in terms of objects, we can think about it in terms of action.

The primary human action is, of course, work. Even in the Garden of Eden, Adam was given a task: to till and keep the garden (Genesis 2:15). When Adam is expelled from the Garden, he is told that work will become toil (Genesis 3:17). But however burdensome it may seem, work too can become an obsession. Since one measure of the value we put on things is the amount of time we give to them, excessive devotion to work can become a form of worship or adoration in its own right. When this happens, we are right back to the problem of treating something in the created order as if it were divine.

It is well known that all the rituals and holidays prescribed by the Torah are second compared to one: a sign between God and the people whereby they are to set aside the demands of the work-a-day world and make room for a special day: Shabbat. It is worth mentioning that the Hebrew word that is usually translated "holy" (*kadosh*) really means separate. If God is separate from the created order, we are asked to honor God by marking off a day that is separate from the rest of the week.

# ◙ Mandating Rest

In the book of Exodus the commandment dealing with Shabbat reads as follows:

> *Remember the Sabbath day, to keep it holy. Six days shalt thou labor, and do all thy work, but the seventh day is a Sabbath unto the Lord thy God; in it thou shalt not do any manner of work, thou, nor thy son, nor thy daughter, nor thy manservant, nor thy maidservant, nor thy cattle, nor thy stranger that is within thy gates; for in six days the Lord made heaven and earth, the sea, and all that in them is, and rested on the seventh day; wherefore the Lord blessed the Sabbath day and hallowed it. (20:8–11)*

According to this passage, Shabbat is supposed to commemorate the creation of the world, but according to

Deuteronomy 5:15 it is supposed to remind us that we were freed from slavery. Putting the two together, we can say that creation and freedom seem to be related: the first has to do with *that* we are here, the second with *why* we are here. In other words, the goal of human life is not endless servitude or slavish devotion to the task of earning a living. As Maimonides points out, the commandment for Shabbat was given *after* the Egyptian captivity, a time when Israel did not work according to free choice and did not have the privilege to refrain from working.[1]

Unfortunately, the commandment dealing with Shabbat is ambiguous. What is meant by refraining from work? Does it mean we are supposed to do nothing? Is refraining from work synonymous with having a good time? If work defines us, if our job is our calling, how do we achieve a higher purpose by staying home? According to Jewish tradition, cessation from work allows one to remember (Exodus 20:8), observe (Deuteronomy 5:12), and take delight (Isaiah 58:13). Normally Shabbat involves a ritual meal, special prayers, study, the experience of pleasure, including physical pleasure, singing, and other forms of entertainment. So while rest (*menuchah*) implies peace and tranquility, it does not necessarily imply indolence. For simplicity, I will interpret rest here in a minimal way, as refraining from all job-related activities and all but the most essential activity, since for many people even a modest amount of rest is an achievement.

The best way to understand rest is to picture what life would be like if there were not a special day set aside for that purpose. We do not have to look upon work as toil to see that a life with nothing *but* work is unfulfilled. In biblical times the primary form of work was food production, a labor-intensive process that involved members of the household, hired hands, slaves, and animals.

Although work in our culture is infinitely more complicated, with relatively few people involved in growing crops or tending herds, there are at least two ways in which our experience is similar to that of people in biblical times. The first is that work is often influenced by forces over which the individual has no control. For a farmer in ancient times, these might include droughts, floods, swarms of insects, or wars; for a modern worker, recessions, mergers, strikes, management shakeups, new regulations, or changes in technology. The second is that work typically involves hierarchical relations. Whether one is dealing with clients, editors, bosses, patients, customers, or colleagues, it is a fact of life that in the workplace, not everyone is equal.

Inequality does not necessarily mean exploitation, and unknown forces sometimes work to people's benefit. Recall that the seven years of famine that brought Jacob to Egypt were preceded by seven years of feast. Still, work brings us face to face with necessity: there are orders to fill, clients to please, reports to write, shipments to make, patients to treat. In some cases there are winners and losers; in practically every case there is the recognition that working is essential for survival.

This does not mean that all work is unpleasant, or

that it is by nature demeaning. We saw that even in the Garden of Eden, Adam had responsibilities. In *Pirke Avot* (2.2), Rabbi Gamaliel maintains that study of the Torah ought to be combined with a worldly occupation lest it lead to sin. For many people work is a calling in the sense that they could not define themselves without it. A life devoted to idleness is almost certainly a life wasted. Shabbat is significant because it represents a contrast with the other six days of the week.

But even if you are lucky enough to view work as a calling, if there is nothing for you but work, there is no getting away from assignments, budgets, social roles, value judgments of other workers, pressure to move upward, and the anxiety of dealing with forces beyond your control. All of this can be very exciting, but if there is no respite, there is no other perspective from which to view the world or your place within it.

As the commandment for Shabbat defines it, rest is not dependent on hierarchical relations. Once work ceases, there are no orders to give and no clients or bosses to please. Thus the commandment for Shabbat states that not only must the heads of the household rest but so must the children, the servants, the stranger, even the animals. On Shabbat all forms of social inequality are dissolved. Instead of parents and children, there are only members of a family; instead of bosses and employees, there are people taking a day off; instead of laborers and beasts of burden, there are creatures enjoying the benefits of leisure. In fact, the Torah goes so far as to say that not only must people and animals rest, but the land must as well. According to Leviticus (25:4) there is supposed to be a *Shabbat Ha-Aretz* (Sabbath of the Earth) every seventh year. Since most people no longer earn their livelihood from the land, we can appreciate the force of this commandment by connecting it with the environment: there are times when even that needs to be taken out of the production cycle and left alone.

What is so important about being left alone? The simple answer is that rest allows a person or a creature to be even more productive when it is time to go back to work. But this reply is too shallow because it assumes that work is the primary goal of life, that we are put on this earth to keep wheels turning and whistles blowing. In short, it assumes that even though God granted us dominion over the animal kingdom, in some respect we too are beasts of burden.

The deeper answer is that we need to be left alone in order to realize that we are not beasts of burden and that there are goals superseding production. As Hermann Cohen put it, the final purpose of life is not realized as long as we remain cogs in civilization's machinery.[2] I offer my own situation as an example. For six days a week I am a professor at a large university. I have classes to teach, books to write, meetings to attend, budgets to keep, and deans to whom I report. Although I am very fond of my job, my role as a professor is not the be-all and end-all of my existence. I therefore insist that as of sundown on Friday I am no longer Professor Seeskin but Ken Seeskin. During Shabbat I do not discuss reading assignments, paper deadlines, or anything else that per-

tains to my responsibilities as a teacher. Rather than being
a teacher or provider, I try to be a husband to my wife, a
father to my children, a son to my parents, and a com-
panion to my friends. It could be said, therefore, that on
this day there is only one thing I can be—myself. I can
look at the whole world and celebrate the fact that God
has decided to make me part of it.

My celebration would be tainted if others had to
work so that I could rest. If that were the case, I would
be no better than a despot living off other people's sweat
and would have little reason to criticize Pharaoh. But the
commandment for Shabbat clearly says that I cannot
have my celebration at someone else's expense. This is
particularly true for the stranger (*ger*), who may be serving as a hired hand. Even if the stranger does not recognize the importance of rest and is a non-Jew, it is
forbidden even to suggest that the stranger perform work
for a Jew on Shabbat.[3] According to Exodus 23:9, Israel
knows the heart of the stranger and cannot take advantage of people living outside their native land. By contrast, a Diaspora Jew cannot force a gentile living in his
or her native land to observe Shabbat if he or she does
not want to. In either case, a non-Jew must be treated with
respect and never subjected to the oppression Israel ex-
perienced in Egypt.[4]

The point is that on Shabbat I cannot judge anyone
on the basis of social role or social status. Rich or poor,
winners or losers in the job market, people who can cope
with outside forces or people who are overwhelmed by
them must all be treated as equals. On this one day I am

asked to recognize that if God created me and allowed me to pursue my own ends, the same is true of others. In fact, the spirit of mutual respect extends not only to the social scale but to the animal kingdom as well. On this day I can look at a horse and see not a tool for greater production but a creature in its own right, an animal with its own dignity and sense of self-worth. The same applies to the environment. I can look upon rivers, lakes, and plots of land not as resources to be exploited but as natural objects to be appreciated. On this day, then, I can see everything in the world as a celebrant in God's creation and can pay it the ultimate compliment, which is simply to let it be.

# The Hard Work of Resting

If Shabbat is a celebration that frees us from the demands of the work-a-day world, there is still one feature that strikes many people as odd: Why make the celebration mandatory? According to the Torah (Exodus 31:14), Shabbat is so important that anyone who profanes it must be put to death. Although no one would go to such lengths today, it is noteworthy that Exodus 31 is concerned primarily with the construction of the Tabernacle. The passage prohibits someone from saying that because work on the Tabernacle is holy, it takes precedence over Shabbat; holy work is still work.

The only time in which the rules for Shabbat can be superseded is when a human life is at stake. According to Maimonides, a doctor may light a fire, slaughter an animal, cook food, or heat water to treat a patient who is seriously ill.[5] If two doctors disagree on how serious the illness is, the one who argues for violating Shabbat wins, because even the *possibility* of endangering life overrides Shabbat. Nor can a doctor say, "I know my patient needs hot water, but since there is only one more hour of Shabbat, I will delay the treatment." On Shabbat, as on all other days, the duty to preserve life is paramount. This duty stands in stark contrast to the practices of pagan religions, where life was often sacrificed to appease the gods.

But the mandatory nature of Shabbat is still problematic. No law requires us to exchange gifts on birthdays or have a good time on New Year's Eve. Why should Shabbat be any different? Why not say that rest, though an excellent idea, is voluntary? The answer is that unless there are high walls protecting a period of rest, the social and economic forces that determine life in the work-a-day world would soon invade it so that instead of rest, we would get yet another day of work.[6] Liberal Jews often object that the laws for Shabbat are so restrictive, and some of the procedures for getting around them so complex, that Shabbat imposes a burden of its own. Is it not easier to throw an electric light switch than to program timers designed to do the same thing? The problem is that while rest may seem like a simple and natural event, it is in fact very difficult to define. This is particularly true if rest is supposed to be celebratory.

Rest is not necessarily the same as convenience. During most of the week we become accustomed to the workplace. We have to get up and go to work so many times that it is often difficult to stay home and put work-related issues out of mind. As a result, for many people the most convenient alternative is to continue to work, if not physically, then psychologically. Understanding this tendency, we can also understand why the Israelites often preferred the modest comforts they had in Egypt to life as a free people in the desert. To someone who has worked as a slave, bondage may be more convenient than freedom.

The need to legislate rest may be stronger now than ever before. According to Juliet Schor, between 1967 and 1987 the average American worker put in 163 hours a year of extra time.[7] That amounts to an entire month of work. What was once true of only medical residents, restaurant owners, and top corporate executives is now true of many others: the nine-to-five job has become a thing of the past. And while it is difficult to estimate exactly what toll these hours take in divorce, substance abuse, child abuse, and heart disease, it is likely that the effects are not good.

Increased time on the job affects not only what people do in the workplace but what they do at home. In fact, workplace and home are merging. Telephones give business associates, customers, clients, and patients increased access to our home lives. It is not uncommon today to have phones in bedrooms, bathrooms, patios, and basements. There are car phones, mobile phones, phones on airplanes, and pay phones on many street corners. Some car and mobile phones even have *two* lines. In one respect, this is all to the good: no matter where you go, you can always get in touch with people. In another respect, however, the availability of phones is disturbing: People can also get in touch with us. As a result, there is almost nowhere to go to escape the pressures of the workplace.

But telephones are just the tip of the iceberg. Fax machines enable people to send business forms or legal documents anywhere there is a telephone. Electronic beepers enable them to contact each other in the few remaining places where phones do not reach. More recently home computers have transformed the workplace to such a degree that many people can put in a full day's work without stepping outside their bedroom. Again, there is a good side to this development: A person no longer has to waste time getting to or from the office. But there is also a bad side: The distinction between the workplace and the home has begun to disappear. A person can now be at work any time of the day or night. And to the degree that business has become international, a person may *have* to be at work at all hours because business centers such as London, Frankfurt, and Tokyo are in different time zones. Even the personal computer has been revolutionized by the introduction of smaller units. A person can now take a computer on an airplane or subway, carry it to lunch, or put in a few extra minutes of work while waiting to see the dentist.

No one doubts that improved communications have made workers more productive; but it is easy to become so awed by technological miracles that the hidden costs go unnoticed. In theory, increased productivity should mean that one can do a job in less time and therefore have more opportunity for leisure. Computers, mobile phones, and Fax machines are all advertised as time-saving devices. But in practice, increased productivity often means one is expected to do more work in the same time rather than the same work in less. So while our standard of living may be higher than that of our parents, in many cases the increase has come at the expense of home and family life as well as the ability to escape the workplace. In today's world, work is everywhere. In many ways we have made our own decision to forsake the Promised Land and return to Egypt. Hard work is not necessarily oppressive, but work without limit is.

The home is another area where time-saving devices were supposed to provide more leisure time, but if Schor is right, improved technology has led to higher expectations in this sector as well.[8] A hundred years ago no one but an aristocrat expected rugs to be cleaned once a week, clothes to be changed every day, lawns to be kept in immaculate condition, and daily meals to include a range of delicacies. Now that these luxuries are within reach of most people, there is enormous pressure to acquire them. Therefore, in addition to having to earn the money to buy a house and fill it with appliances, a family is expected to use them every day. No doubt, comfort is a fine thing, but for many people it is purchased at the expense of freedom.

I am not arguing that there is anything wrong with the comforts of civilization. Nor am I arguing that all work is comparable to slavery. Some work is enlightening, ennobling, even redemptive. People who are out of work often feel that they have been deprived of a basic right. The issue is whether we should allow ourselves to become so ruled by work that there is no time for anything else. *No time for anything else* often means *no ability to put value on anything else*. In this respect, a person obsessed with work is comparable to a person who spends endless hours trying to look like Zeus or Aphrodite. In its own way, work can be another false god, which is to say another testament to human vanity.

Needless to say, Shabbat is not a miracle. It cannot eradicate the desire for material things or correct the injustices that result from social inequality. It cannot set you free if your heart is back on the assembly line. All it can do is provide an atmosphere in which you are encouraged to forget the assembly line and direct your attention to more important matters. As Heschel put it, who we are depends on what Shabbat is for us.[9]

# Time, Space, and God

Shabbat is a unique day set aside to honor a unique God. In biblical times it was a revolutionary idea. No pagan culture had such a day, and some looked upon the idea of mandated rest with contempt.[10] Shabbat is therefore the best way we have to preserve the monotheistic character of our religion, for unlike pagan rituals, in Shabbat there is nothing secret, no element of magic or superstition, and nothing that gives one person an advantage over another. The themes on which Shabbat is based—creation and freedom—are universal in scope and have nothing to do with race, gender, age, social class, or any of the other categories that separate people. According to the Torah, even God rested. That does not mean that God became fatigued after six days of work but rather that rest is a sign of freedom. As Maimonides pointed out, to work from free choice means to have the privilege of refraining from working.

When we compare the concept of sacred time with that of sacred space, it is clear that time enjoys several advantages. As soon as we identify a place as holy, we create the illusion that closeness to God can be measured in inches or miles, that we can court favor with God by getting into an airplane and traveling to a certain location. To make matters worse, location is exclusive: even if a place is big enough to hold thousands of people, a substantial portion of the world's population will never be able to get to it. Time, on the other hand, has no such limitation. Shabbat can be celebrated in Buenos Aires or Katmandu as easily as it can in Jerusalem. As Heschel remarks, God blessed the seventh *day* and called it holy, but there is no reference in the story of creation to God's blessing a physical object or a plot of land.[11]

There is, of course, a tradition in Judaism that regards Jerusalem as a holy city and the Temple Mount as the holiest place in the city.[12] If this is a historical claim about the prayers, rituals, and sacrifices that went on in the Temple, it is certainly true. But if it means, as it often does, that there is an inherent difference between this plot of land and all others, that creation began with Jerusalem, or that people who enter the land of Israel acquire spiritual and intellectual powers they did not have outside it, then it is nothing but another instance of vanity. The difference between the Temple Mount and Mount Olympus should be more than geographic: the latter was the home of a god who was tied to a particular place while the former was the home of a priestly class who worshipped a God with no spatial limitations at all.

In this connection, it is instructive to note that when Solomon dedicated the Temple, he recognized that for all its splendor, it was only a physical object (I Kings 8:27): "But will God actually dwell on earth? Behold, heaven and the heaven of heavens cannot contain Thee; how much less this house that I have built." These words parallel those of the Psalmist:

> *Whither shall I go from Thy spirit?*
> *Or whither shall I flee from Thy Presence?*
> *If I ascend up into heaven, Thou art there;*
> *If I make my bed in the netherworld, behold,*
> *Thou art there.*
> *If I take the wings of the morning,*
> *And dwell in the uttermost parts of the sea;*
> *Even there would Thy hand lead me,*
> *And Thy right hand would hold me.*
> *(Psalms 139:7–10)*

The three major holidays of Pesach, Shavuot, and Sukkot all commemorate events that took place in the wilderness. By contrast, no holiday commemorates the building of the Temple in Jerusalem and no marker indicates where God first spoke to Moses, where Moses received the law, or where he went to die.

Shabbat, an eternal sign between God and the people, cannot be bought or sold, transferred from place to place, or kept away from the less fortunate among us. The whole world could celebrate Shabbat if it wanted to, and no one would get more of it than anyone else. Like kiddish cups, candle holders, and luxurious sanctuaries, Shabbat represents a compromise. It asks for one day out of seven; its promise of a festive meal, physical pleasure, and time to catch up on sleep offers ample reason to celebrate it if the theological arguments are not sufficient. But it is clear that Shabbat involves far less compromise than anything else. In other words, Shabbat is as perfect a symbol as we will ever get.

According to an old tradition, Shabbat is a preview of the world to come—in Platonic terms, a moving image of eternity. But Maimonides goes further, arguing that whoever keeps Shabbat has a *greater* reward in this world than in the next.[13] We can take this statement to mean that it is possible for a finite creature to serve an infinite and transcendent God to the fullest by resting on Shabbat. The irony is that rest does not require heroic exertion or superhuman talent: It is simply an occasion on which you can be yourself.

# CHAPTER FIVE

# How God Becomes Accessible

You are standing this day all of you before the Lord your God: your heads, your tribes, your elders, and your officers, even all the men of Israel, your little ones, your wives, and the stranger that is in the midst of thy camp, from the hewer of thy wood unto the drawer of water; that thou should enter into the covenant of the Lord thy God—and into His oath—which the Lord thy God maketh with thee this day; that He may establish thee this day unto Himself for a people....

Deuteronomy 29:9–12

# ▨ The Presence of God

The previous two chapters took up the question of how people in the created order can bow their heads to something in the divine. This chapter will consider the reverse: how something in the divine order can become accessible to us. If, as Isaiah maintained, our achievements are as nothing when compared to God, how can we feel that we are standing in the presence of God?

The problem is not very acute in a pagan religion, because once we admit that god has physical manifestations, interaction with humans is easy to explain: god comes down to earth to sit with people, fight with them, eat with them, or be eaten by them. Nor is it acute in mystical religions, where people believe they can shed their mortal nature and achieve union with god. Thus paganism and mysticism both solve the problem by saying that something from one order crosses into the other. There are precedents in Judaism for either approach. We have seen, for example, that God's presence (*Shekhinah*) is often described as a physical object that feels pain or dwells with the people. By the same token, Jewish mystics speak of adhesion (*devekut*) to God, which implies that the gap between God and humans is overcome.

For the most part, though, Judaism has resisted the temptation to make God accessible by submerging one realm into the other. As we saw, it also resists the temptation to establish intermediaries. Although the Torah mentions angels, no significant prayers are directed to them and no ceremonies are undertaken to remember them. And unlike a number of pagan religions, Judaism never allowed ancestor worship or communication with the dead. If God becomes accessible to us, it is as a separate and transcendent being; if we stand before God, it is as fallible creatures. But without an intermediary to get between the two, the problem of interaction becomes all the more acute.

We also saw that throughout the prayerbook a wide variety of metaphors are used to explain this relationship: God is a ruler, parent, shepherd, spouse, or employer. If we dig more deeply, however, we will find that one metaphor permeates everything: that God and Israel are partners who have signed a pact or convenant (*berit*) that binds them forever. In the Torah, God establishes a covenant at three decisive moments: after the flood (Genesis 9.1–17), after Abraham leaves the home of his father and travels to the new land (Genesis 15:1–21), and after the Israelites leave Egypt and reach the wilderness of Sinai (Exodus 19.1–6). One advantage of the covenantal relation is that it is conceived in moral rather than spatial terms. To stand in the presence of God is not to occupy a particular location but to abide by the terms of the agreement.

The issue of covenant, in turn, is related to that of freedom. Recall that Judaism is a religion of contrasts. One of the sharpest contrasts is that between Pharaoh's Egypt, where Israel was subjected to slavery, and the Promised Land, where everything in God's creation is allowed to celebrate Shabbat. Idolatry, then, is associated with servitude, either physical or mental, while monotheism is associated with freedom of choice. But this way of looking at religion is complicated by the idea of covenant. Since the covenant consists of a series of commandments, does it not also ask for servitude? And if it does, if every religion asks for servitude to some degree, does it follow that every religion bears traces of idolatry?

In Judaism the issue is complicated even further by a peculiarity of the Hebrew language: the same root (*avad*) is used whether one is talking about slavery to Pharaoh, service to strange gods, or worship of the true God. Of the three types of service, the first two are obviously related: service to strange gods is as futile and demeaning as anything Pharaoh demanded. But many people have protested that considering everything God asks of Israel, service to God is nothing but another form of slavery. The etymological issue leads directly to a religious one: What are we doing when we perform a commandment? If God is infinite and we are finite, if, as Isaiah said, God's ways are not our ways nor God's thoughts our thoughts, then how can the performance of a commandment be anything but submission to the will of a strange and distant force?

# ▨ Service and Slavery: The Traditional View

The traditional answer to these questions is that submission is the whole point of worship. Left to our own devices, we would probably devise laws against murder, lying, and stealing, but it is doubtful that we would prohibit the mixing of milk and meat or require the wearing of fringes. If the only laws we obeyed were those we came up with ourselves, then belief in God would be trivial. The ultimate authority on behavior would be not God but us.

According to the traditional view, then, it is only when we are willing to undergo sacrifice or put up with inconvenience that our loyalty to God can show itself. Recall God's words to Abraham at Genesis 22:2: "Take now thy son, thine only son, Isaac, whom thou lovest, and get thee into the land of Moriah; and offer him there for a burnt-offering." The passage is significant because God asks Abraham to do something Abraham would never think of doing on his own, something he would consider repulsive. If God had asked Abraham to take Isaac to the land of Moriah for a fishing trip, the request would be much easier to fulfill, but it would not be a test of faith.

The lesson to be learned is that faith has to be tested in order to be valid. Recall that the Israelites were not taken to the Promised Land immediately but had to confront the hardships of the desert before redemption was possible. In a similar way, Judaism must contain more than a prohibition against murder and a set of nontaxing rituals. Worship ought to require effort and dedication. If it becomes too easy, if piety was something you could achieve in your spare time, it would be difficult to take seriously.

To carry the traditional view one step further, the lesson of Sinai is that Israel pledged obedience. Thus Exodus 19:8: "All that the Lord hath spoken we will do." If that promise means anything, Israel must accept divine authority. Whatever God commands is obligatory for the simple reason that it derives from an infinite and unimpeachable source. Although we may speculate on why God approves of this or disapproves of that, from a religious perspective the reasons we devise have nothing to do with the binding nature of the commandments: we are obliged to obey whether or not we can find a rationale. According to David Novak, "It is divine offering, not human acceptance, that creates the obligation. . . . Surely, this is the only cogent position Jewish traditionalists can assert."[1]

Although our culture often views obedience in a negative way, traditionalists remind us that we are not talking about submitting to the will of kings, dictators, or government bureaucrats. As Israel's experience in Egypt made clear, human authority can be arbitrary or self-serving. Even if we move beyond Egypt, there is little doubt that humans are fallible: Nations rise and fall, and conceptions of the good life vary widely from one age to the next. Yet through it all, the will of God remains constant. As Joshua (24:15) tells the people at a critical juncture: "If it seems evil to you to serve the Lord, choose this day whom you will serve; whether the gods which your fathers served that were beyond the River, or the gods of the Amorites, in whose land you dwell; but as for me and my house, we will serve the Lord."

To those who object that servitude of *any* kind is opposed to freedom and therefore demeaning to our humanity, traditionalists answer that freedom is not the same as license. A deer in the forest is free in the sense that it lives under no law and can run wherever it pleases. But a moment's reflection will show that if everyone behaved this way, freedom would not be a blessing. In such an environment, every person's freedom would collide with everyone else's, resulting in a war of all against all. The result, as Thomas Hobbes points out, is that there would be no culture, industry, or art because everyone would live in constant fear of everyone else.[2] Why go to the trouble of building a house or designing a factory if someone can take it away from you without fear of reprisal? In the immortal words of Hobbes, life in a state of nature is solitary, poor, nasty, brutish, and short. So while people would be free to do what they want, the struggle for survival would become so intense, and day to day existence so unpleasant, that they might as well be slaves.

It follows that freedom is not opposed to the rule of law; on the contrary, without the rule of law, freedom is meaningless. In religious terms, there can be no Exodus without a Sinai. Another way to see this is to recognize that freedom is not an isolated concept: it presupposes social conditions such as respect for life and property. Thus freedom has both a positive and a negative component: You cannot be free *to* live your life unless you are free *from* the evils inflicted by a state of nature.

What is true on a social level is also true on a personal one. Although a person forced to obey the orders of a dictator is not free, there is more to freedom than lack of external constraint. To be free, a person has to decide what he or she wants in life and have the discipline and intelligence to achieve it. A drifter who wanders from town to town is not necessarily in control of his destiny. Nor is a person whose every wish is governed by greed or jealousy. Note, for example, that we often speak of people who are slaves to passion or addiction. So even though people may act with impunity, if, like Pharaoh, they are locked in a futile struggle and always act contrary to their own interests, they can be as desperate as those in chains.[3] In short, freedom is something a person has to achieve: To get control of your life and shape it in the way you want is much more difficult than running loose in the forest.

To return to the story of the Exodus, the Israelites faced a choice when they left Egypt: they could come together and form a nation or go off in a thousand directions on their own. To form a nation is to introduce the rule of law, which, in turn, is to recognize a source of authority. As Michael Walzer put it: "The Israelite slaves could become free only insofar as they accepted the discipline of freedom, the obligation to live up to a common standard and to take responsibility for their own actions."[4] The question then becomes: Who or what is in charge? Having witnessed the catastrophe that resulted when Pharaoh abused his power, the Israelites decided to become a nation beholden to God.

According to the traditionalist, it is only by living in harmony with God that the presuppositions of freedom can be met. If God created heaven and earth and gave us the gift of life, any system of law opposed to God is bound to fail. Either it will not respect life and property or it will put human life on a futile and self-destructive course. In either case, failure is antithetical to freedom.

While it may seem paradoxical to describe service as the source of freedom, the paradox is dispelled once we recognize that serving God is not like serving clients, employers, or secular rulers. God does not need our help to build bridges, fight wars, or achieve a higher standard of living. Service to God is rather a way of finding and cultivating the noblest part of ourselves. In the words of Deuteronomy 30:19, to serve God is to choose life over death, the blessing instead of the curse. It does not follow that service to God is easy but rather that, unlike slavery, it is never debilitating: a person is never made worse by fulfilling a commandment. Rabbi Gamaliel therefore tells us that we should do God's will as if it were our own so that God might do our will as if it were divine.[5] The secret to controlling our destiny is not to seek independence from God but to follow the pathway God has set before us. That is why service to God is not a form of slavery, and our way of relating to God is not a throwback to idolatry.

# ▨ The Importance of Consent

According to the traditional view, the commandments are obligatory because of their source: they originate with God. Although the traditional view is right in claiming that freedom is not opposed to the rule of law, it oversimplifies revelation and therefore robs Judaism of one of its most distinctive features. Note, for example, that although Abraham is willing to submit to God's will at Genesis 22, he feels free to question it at Genesis 18:23–32. So no matter how superior God may be, submission alone can never be the whole story.

In fact, God does much more than issue instructions. What is peculiar to the Jewish account of revelation is that God not only gives instruction but both needs and asks for human consent. While the commandments may originate in heaven, they do not become binding until they are accepted by creatures on earth.

The difference is critical. Pharaoh never asked for consent. Most law codes in the ancient world were one-sided: The king issued a proclamation telling the people what was expected of them and what would happen if they failed to comply. The miracle of Sinai is that even though God has the power to force compliance, the Torah paints a very different picture: human acceptance is essential.[6] As much as God wants the commandments to be obeyed, Israel must first agree to live by them. In the words of David Hartman: "Self-restraint by the stronger partner is a necessary component of relationships that respect and seek to enhance the sense of worth and dignity of the weaker partner."[7] The upshot is that no matter how obedient we are, it is never quite true that God is our master and we are God's slaves. On the contrary, the parties to a covenant must be free and consent must be mutual.

Although the Torah was written long before the establishment of Anglo-Saxon contract law, there are several respects in which it anticipates that law and tries to ensure that each party retains its dignity. Specifically, there is an offer, a request for acceptance, and an attempt to give consideration. At Exodus 19:4–5 God states the general terms according to which the covenant is supposed to work:

> *You have seen what I did unto the Egyptians, and how I bore you on eagles' wings, and brought you unto myself. Now, therefore, if you will hearken unto My voice, and keep My covenant, then you shall be My own treasure. . . .*

If the people accept the offer, they will be accorded a status that no other people have: they will be led to the Promised Land and made into a holy nation. At the same time, God will be the sole object of worship and will be served in specific ways by a kingdom of priests. Thus God and Israel will be partners trying to complete the work of creation and make the world a better place.

Throughout the Book of Exodus, and later in the Book of Deuteronomy, the themes of offer and acceptance are repeated again and again. When the words are brought to the people, the Torah says that *all* the people answered *together,* agreeing to do everything God asked.

When the Ten Commandments are presented at Exodus 20:2, the theme of consideration is hinted at again: "I am the Lord your God, who brought you out of the land of Egypt, out of the house of bondage."

When the agreement is ratified at Exodus 24, the same themes appear. Moses recounts *all* the words and *all* the ordinances that the Lord has spoken lest the people enter an agreement whose terms they do not understand.[8] Then *all* the people answer with one voice pledging themselves to *all* the words the Lord has spoken. But even this commitment is not enough. Moses writes everything down and reads it back to the people the following day so that they can be sure they understand what they are getting involved in. Again the reply is emphatic: "*All* that the Lord has spoken we will do."

The act of acceptance is commemorated in a ceremony described at Deuteronomy 27. Moses writes down all the words of the law "very clearly" so that Moses and the Levites can proclaim that the people have become consecrated to the Lord.[9] Acceptance of the covenant is enacted yet again at Deuteronomy 29, where, as Walzer points out, the text is even more explicit about Israel's willingness to live under God's law.[10] Instead of saying that all the people accepted, this chapter goes into a lengthy enumeration of who the people are: the heads of tribes, the elders, the officers, all the men, all their wives, the stranger in the camp, including everyone from hewers of weed to drawers of water. From that point on, no one will be able to say his or her voice was not heard.

In the next chapter of Deuteronomy God goes a step

further by pointing out that not only did the people voice agreement but the terms are such that the people can understand what is expected of them *and* do it. According to Immanuel Kant, *ought* implies *can*. A contract that is impossible to interpret or fulfill imposes no obligation. Note, for example, that one of the standard reasons for voiding a contract is that if none of the parties can abide by it, the agreement is a sham. But the covenant between God and Israel is not a sham, because each side is fully capable of honoring it.

In short, the covenant is binding because it is fair. Instead of receiving orders from a superior power, the people have really bound *themselves*. The most favorable contract in the world is not valid until both parties approve it. Thus all the lightning and thunder on Mount Sinai are beside the point. Pagan gods were famous for causing meteorological disturbances, but only the God of Sinai bothered to ask the people what *they* thought.

From a philosophic perspective, the covenant implies even more than mutual acceptance. In addition to agreeing to live by the covenant, each party must recognize that it imposes a binding obligation, that once the agreement is made, it is forbidden to violate it. On what is this recognition based? Clearly it cannot be based on the covenant itself. The covenant would make no sense unless each party already believed that it is wrong to break a promise. In fact, each party not only must believe that breaking promises is wrong but must be assured that the other party believes it too.

# ▣ Standing Forever at Sinai

Any theory based on the notion of contract or consent is open to an obvious question: What if the agreement is broken? What happens to the contract if the offer is made, acceptance is given, but one party fails to live up to the terms?

The problem of compliance is important because, despite all the steps God takes to ensure that the people know what they are doing, each act of acceptance seems to be followed by an act of betrayal. After accepting the covenant at Sinai, the people turn to the Golden Calf (Exodus 32). After the Golden Calf incident, they complain because they do not have enough to eat (Numbers 11). When they first approach the Promised Land, they decide that they are too weak to take it and elect to go back to Egypt and serve Pharaoh (Numbers 14). It is hardly surprising, then, that Moses tells the people that they have been rebellious against God from the day he met them (Deuteronomy 9:24). What is surprising is that the rebellion does not end when the people enter the Promised Land. We can understand how a people wandering in the desert with little or nothing to eat might become unruly, but according to Deuteronomy 31: 16–22, even the generations that live in the land will continue to provoke God and break the covenant. And according to the prophet Ezekiel (18:27–31), the provocations went on and on.

What, then, do we say to the person who claims that

the partnership between God and Israel has been broken? Or, to look at the same point from a different perspective, what do we say to the person who claims that since the contract was not fulfilled, there is no reason why a person living in this day and age should be bound by it?

If everything depended on Sinai alone, there would be little to say except that Israel did not keep its part of the bargain and therefore the partnership is over. But fortunately everything does not depend on Sinai alone, for a close reading of the Torah indicates that Sinai can be repeated, that the covenant reaches forward to every generation and asks it to forget the mistakes of previous generations and make a fresh start.

At Deuteronomy 27:9, for example, God says: "Keep silent, and hear, O Israel; this day thou art consecrated as a people unto the Lord thy God."[11] Readers have long wondered why God would say you are consecrated as a people *this day* when, in fact, consecration occurred years earlier in the Book of Exodus. Surely God has not forgotten what occurred at Sinai. According to the traditional interpretation, *this day* really means *any day;* in short, God offers the covenant again and again.[12] Even if it has been rejected a thousand times, God offers it yet another time in the hope that the people will accept it with conviction. As Immanuel Kant puts it, morality always begins anew.[13] Each day we get up and we face the challenge of trying to be what God intended us to be. And each day, no matter how close we came before, we have to start over again.

Further support for this interpretation can be found

at Deuteronomy 5:3, where Moses tells the people: "The Eternal made not this covenant with our fathers, but with us." Again the passage seems out of place. Why would Moses tell the generation about to enter the Promised Land that God did not make a covenant with their fathers? Rashi suggests that "not with our fathers" should be taken to mean "not with our fathers *alone*."[14] In other words, our ancestors are not the only ones to whom God offered the covenant. The same sentiment is expressed at Deuteronomy 29:13–14: "Nor is it with you alone that I make this covenant and this oath; but with those who are standing here this day before the Lord our God and with those that are not here with us this day." Thus the Torah goes out of its way to emphasize that we too are partners in the Sinai covenant. According to some accounts this passage implies that the soul of every Jew who would ever live was present to hear God's words and voice approval. But we do not have to interpret the passage in a mythological fashion to see the point it is trying to make: Sinai is not a one-time-only event. The act of offering the covenant is an eternal process that is never exhausted: The covenant is offered whenever we are willing to accept it.

To say that Sinai is an eternal process is to say that it is an ideal one not limited by time or space. In principle the covenant is not an agreement between God and the Israelites in the desert but between God and *ideal* Israel, which is to say Israel as it could be, the Israel that understands its duties and aspirations and accepts them without shirking. To the degree that ideal Israel has

not yet been realized, the covenant has not been completely fulfilled.

Complete fulfillment means no compromises or concessions. Throughout this book we have seen that Judaism
does not present monotheism in its pure form: It takes
into account people's need for tangible symbols and
their reluctance to give up idolatry, and it never loses sight
of the historical circumstances in which people find
themselves. It attempts to move people in a direction
that plays down the importance of spatial location or
lavish spectacles, but it resists the temptation to seek an
immediate transformation. Still, with 613 commandments it is easy to forget that the purpose of the Torah
is not just to regulate behavior but to educate it. Perhaps, then, we can look forward to the day when all
traces of paganism, social inequality, and national chauvinism will be removed from the religion and the people will be ready to accept monotheism without
qualifications.

From our perspective, complete fulfillment means
that we look at the commandments not as a set of re-
quirements imposed on us by a strange and distant will
but as a body of wisdom that expresses our own deep-
est convictions about how to live our lives. To para-
phrase Rabbi Gamaliel, it would mean that we do God's
will as if it were our own, because if we understood ourselves better, we would recognize that there is no difference. We saw, for example, that the laws of Shabbat
may seem like an arbitrary restriction on personal freedom when viewed from afar, but upon reflection it be-

comes clear that those laws were meant to ensure that we do not become slaves to social and economic forces but that we have one day when we can be ourselves. What is true of Shabbat is true of the rest of the commandments: What looks like restriction designed to appease God is really a law designed to enhance the quality of human life. The trick is to understand human life well enough for this point to become clear.

# ▓ Uniqueness and Accessibility

Let us return to the issue of accessibility. God enters into a relation with humans by becoming a partner to a covenant. The covenant represents an ideal of human behavior that may take a lifetime to realize. But the important point is that there is nothing in the covenant that compromises God's uniqueness. The qualities on which the agreement is based—fairness, respect, and consideration—have nothing to do with magic, power, wealth, or sexual prowess. More important, the boundary between the divine order and the created one is never crossed. God remains in heaven, the people remain on earth, and when they stand before God to pledge themselves to God, they do so in a desert, without assistance from angels or supernatural creatures, and with no visual contact with God.[15]

The usual criticism of Judaism is that it makes God too distant, too abstract. With two separate realms and no way to cross them, it is difficult for people to have anything concrete on which to focus. According to Hegel, Judaism cannot help but leave people feeling alienated from God.[16] This criticism has some validity. Without a visual image of the divine or a series of intermediaries, God can seem distant, and with distance comes the risk of estrangement. That does not mean that estrangement is inevitable, but it is a recurring problem and is responsible for many compromises and steps backward. On the other hand, the virtue of having no intermediaries is that when the people decide to become partners with God, as they do at Deuteronomy 29, they stand before God and no one else.

# CHAPTER SIX

# Let My People Go

In every generation, you must look upon yourself as if you personally came out from Egypt, as the Bible says: "And thou shalt tell thy children on that day, saying, it is because of what the Lord did for me when I went forth from Egypt."
For it was not only our ancestors whom the Holy One, whose name be praised, redeemed; the Holy One redeemed us too. . . .

The Passover Haggadah

# ▨ Monotheism and Martyrdom

Let us return to the first and second commandments and the idea of a litmus test of Judaism. A familiar theme of this study is that a conception of God is not in a vacuum; in general, God is associated with the things we value the most. A culture that conceives of God as a ferocious animal values strength and terror; a culture that conceives of God as a magician values secrecy and manipulation; a culture that pictures God in its own image values itself. According to the first commandment, the God Jews are asked to worship wants to be known not for strength, power, or beauty but for an act of redemption (Exodus 20:2): "I am the Lord thy God, who brought thee out of the land of Egypt, out of the house of bondage."

Later in the Book of Exodus (34:6–7) God expands on this idea by telling Moses that divinity is to be conceived in terms of mercy, graciousness, slowness to anger, steadfast love, forgiveness, and moral resolve. Thus when the second commandment says, "Thou shalt have no other gods before Me," it means that we should not treat as ultimate any values other than these. And when it says that we should not bow to or serve graven images, it means that we should devote our lives to imitating the moral qualities of God and forget about what God may look like.

It should be clear, then, why Jewish tradition regards the first and second commandments as equal in weight to the entire Torah. If we made redemption the primary goal of our lives, if we devoted every minute of our lives to mercy, graciousness, and the other qualities revealed to Moses, we would have fulfilled the covenant and done everything possible to make the world a better place. It is true, of course, that there are a host of other commandments that comprise the body of Jewish law, but they can all be seen as symbols, reminders, or precepts designed to reinforce the value system summarized in the first two.

As for the *Shema,* thousands of martyrs did not go to their deaths muttering a numerical truism. When they said that God is one, they meant that the God who stands for mercy, graciousness, and the like is special, that nothing in the universe is comparable to this God or can take the place of this God. They meant, in other words, that Judaism demands a life devoted to these values. That is why they are willing to die rather than abandon them.

From our standpoint, the *Shema* is not an affirmation as much as a challenge. Do we really mean that God is one in this sense? Are we ready to commit ourselves to these values and this life and to regard everything else as secondary? This is another way of asking whether we are willing to resist the temptation to serve the gods of wealth, fame, beauty, and power, recognizing that they are not gods at all but human shortcomings disguised as gods.

# The Long Road to Monotheism

From whatever angle you view it, idolatry is a complex and deep-seated problem that will not go away easily. Certainly it will not go away merely by our repeating the six words of the *Shema*. The main question posed by this study is how to combat a problem that is as old as history itself and rears its head in every age.

Although there are biblical passages that suggest that idolatry can be eliminated all at once if people are vigilant enough (e.g., Deuteronomy 7:1–5), the normal approach is not to seek an immediate solution but to recognize that a small step is better than no step at all.[1] In some cases Judaism borrowed pagan rituals but invested them with a new meaning. Harvest festivals that once glorified nature became Pesach, Shavuot, and Sukkot, festivals that commemorate redemption from slavery and revelation at Sinai. The practice of killing the firstborn male became the practice of redeeming the firstborn male by "buying it back" from God.[2] In other cases Judaism catered to the people's need for tangible symbols by offering them the Tabernacle, priestly vestments, and the Temple in Jerusalem. In still others, it found expression in a literature that contains fanciful imagery and scores of anthropomorphic descriptions.

The rationale for making concessions is that rather than ask people to approach monotheism on a take-it-or-leave-it basis, the tradition allows them to approach it in stages. To borrow an allegory from Plato, a person who lived in a cave and was suddenly thrust into daylight would find it hard to see until her eyes became accustomed to the new surroundings.[3] We can even imagine her wanting to go back down where the light was less intense. If we took her and forced her to look at the sun right away, she might well go blind. But if we moved in a slower fashion, allowing her to look skyward a bit more each day, she would have a much better chance to see what the world outside the cave is like.

What is true of the sun is also true of God. Expose people to the idea of uniqueness right away and they are likely to balk. Who is this God? Where can I find God? That is why the tradition begins with ideas that are easier to accept. Observe the festivals, say the prayers, eat the foods, allow yourself to be moved by the beauty of the sanctuary, and *then* you will be in a position to appreciate the worldview that underlies them. The anthropomorphic descriptions of God are valuable up to a point. We need them to call on God, direct attention to God, and make a place for God in our lives; but calling on God is one thing, understanding the unique character of God another. The tradition teaches us that you have to do the former before you can be expected to do the latter.

What is true on an individual level is also true on a historical one. Just as the understanding of idolatry changed from one age to the next, the idea of monotheism did as well. In biblical times monotheism was closely associated with the birth of a nation and the establishment of a priestly cult. The prohibition against making images of God was quite specific: it referred to graven images like the ones used by other nations. In the Rabbinic period politics and religion became separated when people realized that the idea of monotheism could survive without a priesthood, a Temple in Jerusalem, or a homeland. In the medieval period monotheism became the foundation of a philosophic system that attempted to unite the teachings of the prophets with the thought of Plato and Aristotle. Notice how the idea changed. Although Maimonides claims that the prophets were sophisticated philosophers in their own right, there is no historical evidence to back him up. In all likelihood the prophets would have had no appreciation of the intricate theories that Maimonides thought monotheism entailed.

A similar argument could be made for a secular idea such as democracy. To an ancient Athenian, democracy did not involve separation of church and state but did mean active participation in the affairs of government. To the founders of the U.S. Constitution democracy was compatible with slavery. Today the average American citizen probably does not participate in the affairs of government but believes in religious freedom and abhors slavery. So whether we are in a religious context or a secular one, great ideas do not come upon the scene all at once. On the contrary, it may take centuries for the full implications of an idea to be worked out.

When we look at Judaism in its current form, we must keep in mind that it too is part of the evolutionary process. This means that it must balance the need for continuity with previous generations against the need to stay current with new ones. Once again, there is a powerful argument for gradualism. Perhaps the full implications of monotheism will not be known until the end of days. Perhaps there are implications that many of us would be shocked to learn if a prophet were to reveal them all at once. It is even possible that if we learned of some of these implications, many people would leave the religion unless it took a couple of steps backward.

The problem with gradualism is that it often becomes an excuse for standing still. We can talk about the meaning of the *Shema,* but first let us have one more dinner dance, one more Torah cover, one more nameplate, and one more sermon on why God is our friend and takes our side in every dispute. No matter how slowly it moves, progress requires that we shed one set of ideas and adopt another. But whether we are talking about Jews, Muslims, Christians, or Buddhists, many people turn to religion not to consider new ideas but to seek confirmation for old ones. Rituals that were intended to awaken a deeper interest in the religion become occasions for feeling comfort or relaxation; what was once a concession becomes an end in itself. The idea of a litmus test for Judaism makes sense only if effort is required to pass the test.

# Conclusion: What It Means to Be a Jew

Now that all the passages have been cited and arguments made, it is time to take stock. In a legal sense, Judaism is a nationality defined by birth or conversion. In a deeper sense, though, Judaism has always understood itself as a nation with a purpose. That purpose was expressed by Steven S. Schwarzschild in the bluntest possible way: The world is lousy and ought to be made better.[4] In theological terms, the world is redeem*able* but as yet unredeemed.

If the world were satisfactory just as it is, there would be no need to look for a source of value beyond the world. From a Jewish perspective, however, human consciousness begins with the recognition that things are not as they should be: children starve, innocent people suffer, minorities are oppressed, and men and women try to settle their disputes by resorting to violence. The reason God cannot resemble anything in the world is that no person, government, or institution is so exalted that it can serve as a point of comparison. So our basic sense that injustice needs to be corrected presupposes a moral authority that has no taint of injustice itself: a God who is more than a human projection, a God who is unique.

Unless the world were redeem*able*, there would be no point in trying to make it better. Confronted with starving children and innocent suffering, we would have to accept things as they are. Throughout the Torah, God implores us to improve on what we have and heaps blame on us when we do not. On the other hand, if the world were already redeemed, there would be nothing left to do but acknowledge its greatness and congratulate ourselves. At its core, Judaism is opposed to anything that smacks of complacency. We saw that just before the people have completed 40 years of wandering and are ready to enter the Promised Land, Moses warns them that they have been rebellious in the past and have no reason to feel smug about the future.[5] The problem with complacency is that it leads to inactivity. To be a Jew is to accept obligation, undertake a task, and be willing to rededicate yourself if the efforts to complete the task fail.

The task of making the world better requires that we do not regard it as ultimate in its present state. It also requires that we recognize that appealing to narcissism, magic, or uncritical assessments of human achievement will not help, and in all probability will make matters worse. On the positive side, the task of making the world better requires that we accept the contrasts Judaism gives us, separating physical appearance from moral worth, seeing beyond the social boundaries that keep people apart, and establishing institutions based on consent rather than on obedience to authority. Although the struggle against false gods has been going on ever since Abraham left his father's house and set out for a new land, Judaism offers hope that one day our efforts will succeed and false gods of every description will lose their appeal. On that day we will complete our exodus from Egypt in every sense of the term. We will leave behind us not only Pharaoh but the values Pharaoh stood for: flesh pots, autocratic rule, black magic, lavish shrines, and endless work. On that day, we will be able to see ourselves as full participants in redemption and bow our heads when we hear, "I am the Lord thy God. . . ."

# Appendix

## The Golden Calf:
## A Concession that Did Not Work

Although the Golden Calf (Exodus 32) is often viewed as a paradigm case of idolatry, the text is more ambiguous than is generally thought. After Moses is delayed on the mountain, the people ask Aaron to build a god (*elohim*) for them. Aaron collects a pile of gold jewelry and recasts it in the shape of a calf. When the people see the statue, they respond by saying, "This is your god [*elohim*], O Israel, which brought you out of the land of Egypt." Aaron responds by building an altar and proclaiming that there will be a festival to the Lord the following day. At the festival, the people eat, drink, play, and bring sacrifices.

The passage is puzzling for a variety of reasons. In the first place, the word *elohim* can refer to: (1) the true God (Genesis 1:1), in which case it takes a singular verb; (2) false gods (Exodus 20:3), angels, or heavenly creatures; or (3) anyone who exercises legal or moral authority

(Exodus 4:16; 21:6). So when the people ask Aaron to make them *elohim,* it is not clear whether they are trying to worship a new god, asking for a graven image of the God of Israel, or asking for a tangible symbol to rally the people in Moses' absence. Note, for example, that after building the statue, Aaron does not say that there will be a pagan rite but rather a festival to the Lord. Still, Psalm 106 (19–20) tells us that the people exchanged the glory of God for the image of a bull.

Rabbinic commentators such as Rashi and Nachmanides try to take the sting out of the passage by arguing that the people wanted not a new god but something infused with the spirit of the God of Israel to take the place of Moses. By saying that there would be a festival to the Lord on the following day, Aaron was playing for time: He thought that if he could keep the people occupied for another 24 hours, it was likely that Moses would return. Moreover, the statement, "This is *your* god, O Israel" indicates that the people at fault were not the Israelites themselves but the "mixed multitude" (Exodus 12:38) of prisoners, beggars, and street people who also took part in the exodus. If the culprit had been the Israelites themselves, the text would have read "This is *our* God." Rashi therefore concludes that when God says to Moses, "Go down, for your people, whom you brought out of Egypt, have corrupted themselves" (Exodus 32:7), it is the mixed multitude who are being criticized, as well as Moses for allowing them to join the Israelites.

What are we to make of the passage? I am unsympathetic with the attempt to blame the problem on "outside agitators." Recall that the general drift of Rabbinic commentary is that idolatry is a social problem caused by association with other peoples. Elsewhere in the Torah (Numbers 11:4), when the mixed multitude are responsible for a problem, the text clearly says so. But there is no such reference at Exodus 32, and even if outsiders started the trouble, the clear implication is that it soon became widespread. What is more, in Deuteronomy 31, not to mention the writings of the prophets, it is apparent that idolatry was a problem for the entire Israelite nation. Perhaps Rashi was responding to the Christian view (Acts 7:39–40), according to which the Golden Calf constitutes Israel's breaking of the covenant.[1] Against this view, however, it is noteworthy that the covenant is reestablished several times before the Torah ends.

Whether the people were asking for an image of the true God or a rallying point to replace Moses, the fact remains that the sin is so great that God threatens to destroy them in the desert. Thus Exodus 32:30: "You have sinned a great sin." Recall that the second commandment prohibits *both* the worship of other gods *and* the making of graven images for religious purposes, so the Golden Calf appears to be a violation of the commandment in some form or other. According to Sarna, there are good grounds for linking the sin of the Golden Calf to adultery.[2] If so, the passage would be in keeping with the general tendency to associate idolatry with infidelity.

On the choice of a calf or young bull, there is no doubt that this image was widespread in the ancient world (I Kings 12:28; Hosea 8:5). Note, however, that the qualities normally associated with bulls, such as strength, aggression, and fertility, stand in marked contrast to the qualities revealed to Moses at Exodus 34:6–7.

Finally, there is the issue of Aaron's participation in the whole affair. It was, after all, Aaron who made the statue, built an altar in front of it, and allowed the people to make sacrifices to it. When Moses confronts him, Aaron tries to avoid responsibility by saying that he threw the gold into the fire and the statue popped out as if by magic (Exodus 32:24). According to Deuteronomy 9:20, God was so angry with Aaron that God wanted to destroy him along with the rest of the people. Whether Aaron was a full participant or just stalling for time, he made concessions to the people and allowed them to get out of control (Exodus 32:25). Here, then, is a concession that ends in disaster. Moses, the prophet, insists on adherence to the second commandment, while Aaron, the priest, gives in to the people's need for an idol.

If there is a moral to the story, it is that concessions are not always needed, and in some cases ought to be avoided. Although we cannot adhere to strict monotheism all the time, there are times when we have to take the hard road and be willing to put up with inconveniences.

# Notes

CHAPTER ONE

# Why Idolatry
# Is Alive and Well

1. See Rashi's commentary on Exodus 19:19 and Maimonides, *Guide of the Perplexed,* 2.33.

2. *Megillah* 13a.

3. *Yoma* 69b.

4. For an excellent discussion of the different conceptions of idolatry, see M. Halbertal and A. Margalit, *Idolatry,* trans. N. Goldblum (Cambridge, MA: Harvard University Press, 1992).

5. The comparison between idolatry and infidelity is a prominent feature of Deuteronomy 31:16–21. Also see Exodus 34:15, Hosea 1–3, Isaiah 1:21, Jeremiah 3:1, 4:30–31.

6. Maimonides, *Guide of the Perplexed,* 1.36. For further discussion of Maimonides' view, see Kenneth Seeskin, *Maimonides: A Guide for Today's Perplexed* (West Orange, NJ: Behrman House, 1991), pp. 3–11, 19–23.

7. Maimonides, *Mishneh Torah,* Laws on Idolatry 1.1–2.

8. A. J. Heschel, *Between God and Man* (New York: The Free Press, 1959), p. 102.

9. *Guide of the Perplexed,* 1.57.

10. Hermann Cohen, "Uniqueness Rather Than Unity," in *Reason and Hope,* ed. Eva Jospe (New York: W. W. Norton, 1971), pp. 90–94. Cohen's position is, of course, a statement of Maimonides'. See *Guide* 1.57.

11. Isaiah's words call to mind Exodus 15.11.

12. *Pirke Avot* 2:21.

13. See, for example, Genesis 3:8: "And they heard the voice of the Lord God walking in the garden . . . " and 3:22: "Behold, the man has become like one of us. . . ."

14. For the *Shekhinah* in exile with the Jewish people, see *Megillah* 29a. For its presence or departure from a house of worship, see *Exodus Rabbah* 2.2 and *Numbers Rabbah* 1.3, 13.6. For the presence of the *Shekhinah* with the righteous, see *Sotah* 17a; *Pirke Avot* 3.7. For the *Shekhinah* in pain or experiencing emotion, see *Sanhedrin* 46a and *Sotah* 5a. These and similar passages are surveyed in J. Abelson, *The Immanence of God in Rabbinic Literature* (London: Macmillan, 1912). For a more recent discussion of the issue, one that criticizes some of Abelson's conclusions, see E. Urbach, *The Sages,* 2nd ed., trans. I. Abrahams (Jerusalem: Magnes Press, 1979), Chapter 3. Note, as Urbach does (p. 63), that the *Shekhinah* is not a separate entity existing alongside God but a way of thinking of the nearness or presence of God. In a word, the *Shekhinah* is not an intermediary. For another recent discus-

sion that reaches a similar conclusion, see Steven S. Schwarzschild, "*Shekhinah* and Eschatology," in *The Pursuit of the Ideal,* ed. M. Kellner (Albany, NY: SUNY Press, 1990), pp. 235–250.

15. *Zohar* 1.22a. For sexual connotations of the *Shekhinah,* see Gershom Scholem, *Major Trends in Jewish Mysticism* (1941; repr. New York: Schocken Press, 1961), pp. 225–235. Note, however, that these connotations are found in the mystical tradition, not canonical literature. On this point, see Urbach, *The Sages,* pp. 64–65. But a more recent study by Elliot R. Wolfson, *Through a Speculum That Shines* (Princeton: Princeton Univ. Press, 1994) argues that anthropomorphism has a strong foothold in Jewish tradition. With anthropomorphism comes sexual imagery of all kinds.

16. For the desire to return to slavery, see Exodus 16. 2–3, 17.3; Numbers 11.4–6, 1-3.

---

**CHAPTER TWO**

# The Idol and Its Allure

1. The most prominent exception to the way Greek gods are portrayed is Hephaestus, who is lame and often a subject of ridicule.

2. Why, then, does Genesis 1:26 say that man is made in God's image (*tzelem*)? The answer has to be that in this passage, "image" cannot mean physical likeness and has to mean something more abstract. Thus we say "He was the image of valor" without implying

that valor has two arms and two legs. According to Maimonides (*Guide of the Perplexed,* 1.1), all that Genesis 1:26 means is that God endowed humans with reason. Note that similar problems arise in regard to Isaiah 6:1–2 and Ezekiel 1:26–29 *if* we insist on literal interpretation. According to Maimonides, literal interpretation of every passage in the Bible makes idolatry unavoidable. I will have more to say on this issue in the last chapter.

3. For further discussion of Exodus 33, see *Guide,* 1.37 and Kenneth Seeskin, *Maimonides: A Guide for Today's Perplexed* (West Orange, NJ: Behrman House, 1991), pp. 34–37.

4. On gender roles, see Isaiah 42:14, where God is compared to a woman in labor. For a recent discussion of the tendency for monotheism to become monolatry (worship of a male god), see Judith Plaskow, *Standing Again at Sinai* (San Francisco: Harper and Row, 1990), Chapter 4.

5. Yehezkel Kaufmann, *The Religion of Ancient Israel,* trans. and abridged by M. Greenberg (New York: Schocken, 1972), pp. 40–42, 80–81.

6. Nahum Sarna, *Exploring Exodus* (New York: Schocken Books, 1986), p. 58.

7. On the folly of magic, see, for example, Hosea 4:12, 10:15, 13:2; Isaiah 17:8, 47:9–12; Zephaniah 1:4–6; Jeremiah 7:17–18, 44:15–21; Ezekiel 8:20, 20:32; II Maccabes 12:40.

8. For an excellent discussion of Jewish superstitions, see Joshua Trachtenberg, *Jewish Magic and Superstition: A Study in Folk Religion* (New York: Behrman House, 1939). Note how persistent superstition is despite all the attempts to ban or discredit it.

9. Kaufmann, *Religion of Ancient Israel,* p. 53.

10. See *Guide,* 1.58–59 and Seeskin, *A Guide for Today's Perplexed,* pp. 27–34.

11. *Guide,* 1.32.

12. *Guide,* 1.58.

---

# CHAPTER THREE

# Sacred Space

1. A cubit represents the distance from the tip of the middle finger to the point of the elbow, approximately 18 to 20 inches. For color pictures of a miniature re-creation of the Tabernacle, see Moshe Levine, *The Tabernacle* (New York: Soncino Press, 1989).

2. According to Exodus 12:35–36, the gold and jewelry for the Tabernacle were taken from the Egyptians.

3. Naham Sarna, *Exploring Exodus* (New York: Schocken Press, 1986), p. 196.

4. The Hebrew word *shakhon* (to dwell) is the root from which we derive *Shekhinah* (the indwelling presence of God). Thus Exodus 29:45: "And I will dwell among the children of Israel and will be their God."

5. For another description of the cherubim, see Ezekiel 1:4–14, where the prophet pictures them with four wings and four distinct faces.

6. Sarna, *Exploring Exodus,* p. 213.

7. Solomon Schecter, *Some Aspects of Rabbinic Theology* (New York: Schocken Press, 1975), p. 292.

8. Maimonides, *Guide of the Perplexed,* 1.31.

9. *Guide,* 3.32.

10. For an excellent discussion of Jewish esthetics in general and the *Shulchan Aruch's* laws on forms and images in particular, see Steven S. Schwarzschild, "The Legal Foundation of Jewish Aesthetics," in *The Pursuit of the Ideal,* ed. M. Kellner (Albany, NY: SUNY Press, 1990), pp. 109–116.

---

CHAPTER FOUR

# Sacred Time

1. Maimonides, *Guide of the Perplexed,* 2.31.

2. Hermann Cohen, "Affinities Between the Philosophy of Kant and Judaism," in *Reason and Hope,* trans. Eva Jospe (New York: W. W. Norton, 1971), p. 8.

3. On the issue of strangers performing work, see *Shabbat* 16.6–8;

Maimonides, *Mishneh Torah,* Book Three, Laws of Shabbat 6. For further discussion, see David Novak, *Jewish Social Ethics* (New York: Oxford University Press, 1992), pp. 143–152.

4. References to the rights of the stranger assume, of course, that the stranger does not express contempt for Judaism or endanger the welfare of Jews. According to tradition, the maximum that can be required of the stranger is compliance with the seven Noachide commandments, which prohibit idol worship, blasphemy, murder, adultery, stealing, and eating flesh cut from a live animal, and require courts of justice. The reason is that any command given to Noah is binding on the whole human race.

5. Maimonides, *Mishneh Torah,* Book Three, Laws of Shabbat 2.13.

6. I owe the wall metaphor to Leo Baeck, *The Essence of Judaism,* trans. Grubenwieser and Pearl (New York: Schocken Books, 1961), p. 145.

7. Juliet B. Schor, *The Overworked American* (New York: Basic Books, 1992), p. 29.

8. Schor, *Overworked American,* p. 85.

9. A. J. Heschel, *The Sabbath* (New York: Farrar, Straus, Giroux, 1951), p. 89. For a similar study of more recent vintage, see Pinchas H. Peli, *The Jewish Sabbath* (New York: Schocken Books, 1988).

10. For pagan contempt for Shabbat, see Novak, *Jewish Social Ethics* p. 145.

11. A. J. Heschel, *Between God and Man* (New York: The Free Press, 1959), pp. 214–218.

12. For the tradition that regards the city of Jerusalem as holy, see *Kelim* 1:7–8. For a sobering commentary on this passage, see Yeshayahu Leibowitz, *Judaism, Human Values, and the Jewish State,* trans. Eliezer Goldman (Cambridge; MA: Harvard University Press, 1992), pp. 86–87.

13. *Mishneh Torah,* Book Three, Laws of Shabbat 30:15.

---

CHAPTER FIVE

# How God Becomes Accessible

1. David Novak, *Jewish Social Ethics* (New York: Oxford University Press, 1992), p. 36.

2. Thomas Hobbes, *Leviathan,* 1.13.

3. For a classic expression of the argument that license can be confining, see Plato, *Republic,* 577e, where the tyrant is described as a being slave to his own passions and having less freedom than anyone in the city.

4. Michael Walzer, *Exodus and Revolution* (New York: Basic Books, 1985), p. 53.

5. *Pirke Avot* 2.4.

6. According to *Shabbat* 88a, God held a mountain over the heads of the people and threatened to drop it on them if they did not accept the convenant. The problem is, as the rabbis recognized, that if someone enters an agreement under coercion, the agreement is void. I interpret this passage as an expression of God's eagerness to have Israel enter the covenant, not a statement of literal truth.

7. David Hartman, *A Living Covenant* (New York: The Free Press, 1985), p. 24.

8. For the terms of the agreement, see Exodus 24:7: "We will do and [then] listen" is sometimes taken to mean that the people agreed to follow God *before* they knew what God would ask of them. See, for example, *Shabbat* 88a. Note, however, that this passage occurs after the Ten Commandments and a number of other commandments have been revealed. So all the people could be saying is that they will do and then listen to that portion of the law that has yet to be revealed (on this point, see Rashi's commentary). It is also worth noting that throughout Exodus and Deuteronomy the people are given ample opportunity to *withdraw* their acceptance if they want to. My own interpretation is that the passage is an expression of deep commitment rather than blind faith. Thus, we will hear not in a dispassionate way but with the expressed *intent* of doing. The appropriate analog is a marriage vow, where expectations run high but the agreement is still legally binding.

9. For an interesting discussion of the ratification ceremony, see Emmanuel Levinas, "The Pact," in *The Levinas Reader,* ed. S.

Hand (Oxford, England: Basil Blackwell, 1989), pp. 211–26. According to Levinas, there were 603,550 Israelites at Sinai and 48 ratifications described in the Torah, so even at an elementary level, the covenant was ratified 28,970,400 times.

10. Walzer, pp. 75–76.

11. Compare Deuteronomy 11:16 and 11:32, where practically the same language is employed.

12. *Berakhot* 63b.

13. Immanuel Kant, *The Metaphysics of Morals,* 6:409.

14. Rashi, Deuteronomy 32.

15. Hermann Cohen, *Religion of Reason Out of the Sources of Judaism,* trans. Simon Kaplan (New York: Frederick Ungar Publishing, 1972), pp. 76–78. There are, of course, passages where Moses functions like an intermediary. In the Book of Exodus he is alone with God on the mountain; in Exodus (20:15–18) and Deuteronomy (5:23–27) he brings God's word to the people because they are afraid they will die if they hear it. That is why it is important that Moses, among the meekest of men (Numbers 12:3), is a teacher of God's will rather than a demi-god in his own right. In fact, Moses is a sinner (Deuteronomy 32:51) whose life ends in tragedy when he is not allowed to enter the Promised Land. So even though he was the greatest prophet Israel will ever produce, in the last analysis, he is only human.

16. Georg Wilhelm Friedrich Hegel, *Lectures on the Philosophy of Religion,* Vol. Two, Second Division, Section 1.

CHAPTER SIX

# Let My People Go

1. On the issue of the small step being better than no step at all, see Michael Walzer, pp. 144–49.

2. On "buying back" the firstborn male, see Exodus 13:2, 13:12–13; Numbers 3:13, 18:15–16.

3. Plato, *Republic,* 514 ff.

4. Steven S. Schwarzschild, "An Agenda for Jewish Philosophy in the 1980's," in *Studies in Jewish Philosophy,* ed. N. Samuelson (Lanham, MD: University Press of America, 1987), p. 108.

5. Deuteronomy 9:6, 9:24, 31:16–22, 31:27.

---

APPENDIX

# The Golden Calf:
# A Concession That Did Not Work

1. For more on post-biblical interpretation see L. Smoler and M. Aberbach, "The Golden Calf Episode in Postbiblical Literature," *Hebrew Union College Annual* 39 (1968) pp. 91–116.

2. Sarna, pp. 219–220.

# Index